Experiences of Grassroots Development

In recent years one of the sources of modest optimism in development has been the growth in number and positive impact of indigenous, non-governmental organisations working in communities at local level. Zed Books has, therefore, launched a new series of books which examines these concrete experiences with a view to the lessons that can be learned for participatory, gender-sensitive and environmentally sustainable development.

Kalima Rose
WHERE WOMEN ARE LEADERS
The SEWA Movement in India
(1993)

Manfred Max-Neef
FROM THE OUTSIDE LOOKING IN
Experiences in 'Barefoot Economics'
(reissued 1993)

Susan Holcombe
MANAGING TO EMPOWER
The Grameen Bank's Experience of Poverty Alleviation
(1995)

Zachariah and Sooryamoorthy
SCIENCE IN PARTICIPATORY DEVELOPMENT
Achievements and Dilemmas of a Development Movement
(1994)

Md. Anisur Rahman
PEOPLE'S SELF-DEVELOPMENT
Perspectives on Participatory Action Research
(1993)

Craig and Mayo (eds)
COMMUNITY EMPOWERMENT
A Reader in Participation and Development
(1995)

Managing to Empower

THE GRAMEEN BANK'S EXPERIENCE OF
POVERTY ALLEVIATION

ABOUT THE AUTHOR

Susan Holcombe brings diverse experiences to an analysis of the management of a bank that by mid-1994 was serving nearly two million poor clients in rural Bangladesh. She has worked with former New York State Assemblyman Oliver Koppell on housing problems in the Bronx in New York City and on public authorities in New York State. She has worked with UNICEF in Afghanistan, Pakistan, Fiji and Sudan on programs aimed at expanding primary health care services. She has become increasingly concerned with the effects of poverty on people's capacity to demand and use health and other government services, and with the capacities of government extension services to reach the rural poor. She worked with UNIFEM on strategic planning and organization development efforts that helped transform the scope and capacity of that organization. Most recently she has been working in China with UNFPA in support of efforts to make fundamental improvements in the quality of MCH and family planning services at the grassroots in 305 poor counties. A graduate of Mount Holyoke College, she holds an M.P.I.A. from the Graduate School of Public and International Affairs at the University of Pittsburgh and a Ph.D. from New York University's Wagner School of Public Service.

Managing to Empower

THE GRAMEEN BANK'S EXPERIENCE OF POVERTY ALLEVIATION

Susan Higinbotham Holcombe

With a Foreword by
JAMES GUSTAVE SPETH
Administrator, the United Nations Development Programme

UNIVERSITY PRESS LIMITED
Dhaka

ZED BOOKS
London & New Jersey

Managing to Empower:The Grameen Bank's Experience of Poverty Alleviation was first published by Zed Books Ltd, 7 Cynthia Street, London N1 9JF, UK , and 165 First Avenue, Atlantic Highlands, New Jersey 07716, USA, in 1995.

The Bangladesh edition was published by Mohiuddin Ahmed, The University Press Ltd, Red Crescent Building, 114 Motijheel C/A, PO Box 2611, Dhaka 1000, Bangladesh in 1995.

Cover design by Andrew Corbett
Printed and bound in the United Kingdom by
Redwood Books, Trowbridge, Wiltshire

A catalogue record for this book is available from the British Library.
US CIP data is available from the Library of Congress.

ISBN 1 85649 315 6 Hb
ISBN 1 85649 316 4 Pb
Dhaka ISBN 984 05 1292 7

CONTENTS

ACKNOWLEDGEMENTS

The field research on which this book is based and its publication would not have been possible without the support and encouragement of several institutions and individuals.

Thanks goes first of all to Grameen Bank staff whose openness to discussion of all issues and willingness to facilitate arrangements made it possible to begin to understand the management of a large poverty alleviation organization. Professor Muhammad Yunus, the founder and Managing Director of Grameen Bank, was patient with questions and generous with his time. His commitment to the work of the Bank coupled with a belief in the capacities of people are mirrored in many of the Bank staff. Senior Managers in Dhaka set aside time for interviews and helped to supply data requested. Ms. Maheen Sultan, Resource Person in the Grameen Secretariat, took great pains to organize a complicated field schedule and to set up interviews with Head Office staff. The Area Managers observed opened their offices, homes, and hearts to the researchers. Branch Managers, Bank Assistants and Bank members were unfailingly courteous and helpful, if curious as to why a middle-aged American woman was venturing into the far reaches of Bangladesh. Bangladesh can have no better advertisement than its people who live and work in rural areas.

Zahidul Islam was an able research assistant and cheerful companion in field work. Angela van Rynbach provided an opportunity to observe the field operations of an international NGO in Bangladesh (Save the Children U.S.). Denise Conway and Hedy and Wolfgang Fischer offered friendship and support in Bangladesh.

Equally the research would not have been possible without the support of Mount Holyoke College which awarded a Hannum-Warner Travel Fellowship to cover the costs of travel to and inside Bangladesh and the costs of the research assistant. A grant from the Elsie Elfring Higinbotham Fund supports distribution of the book in Bangladesh.

Finally thanks are due to those who gave guidance to the research, who patiently read original drafts and recommended streamlining and clarification, or who assisted in preparation of the text. They include Roy Sparrow, Sonia Ospina, Demetrios Argyriades, Howard Bloom, Zora Sabov, Rebecca Holcombe, and Arthur Holcombe.

Susan H. Holcombe

FOREWORD

The tale of Grameen Bank is by now a familiar one - the phenomenal repayment rate (in excess of 98 percent); the documented ability to reach more than ten million poor, rural households in Bangladesh with the small loans (the equivalent of $60 - 70 on average) that can make such a difference to family well-being and self-sufficiency; the measurable improvement in income and assets of borrower-members, 91 percent of whom are women. This is the success story of a curious hybrid of a commercial bank **and** an organization dedicated to alleviating rural poverty.

How did these celebrated achievements come about? What management structures are behind its well-publicized success? Susan Holcombe provides valuable insights into the workings of Grameen - insights that those who seek to export the Grameen model would do well to bear in mind.

This study emerges against a backdrop of renewed debate about the future of international cooperation for development. Since 1988, overseas development assistance has barely kept pace with development. Many, if not most, of the Northern industrial countries are actively debating a retrenchment of their international involvement. The threat comes from many sources, including aid fatigue, competing domestic priorities, sluggish economies, and lack of public understanding.

Ironically, even as international support for development is under attack, perhaps as never before, the magnitude of the challenge continues to increase. Today, an estimated 13 - 18 million people die from hunger, malnutrition and poverty-related causes every year. That is the equivalent of 100 fully loaded jumbo jets crashing daily. Bangladesh has not been spared from this tragedy.

The challenges of poverty, hunger and malnutrition in Bangladesh - and the rest of the developing world - will not be met by more of the same, even a lot more. Something new is needed, a new paradigm of development, an approach that goes by many names, but one that we at UNDP call **sustainable human development**. The work of Grameen Bank in many ways embodies the best of this approach. Sustainable human development is first and foremost **people-centered**, putting poor people first and meeting their basic needs. As Susan Holcombe shows us, Grameen has turned the usual model of banking on its head, taking its services to the village and the people, rather than asking them to come to Grameen.

Sustainable human development also is **participatory**, ensuring that people have a share in the decisions that shape their lives. Ms. Holcombe takes us inside the management culture of Grameen, showing how a framework of shared vision and values has enabled Grameen to build a system that brings borrower-members into decision-making roles, and motivates a large and widely dispersed field staff to turn in a level of consistent, honest performance that amazes many observers.

The events we read of daily can make us feel that the world as we know it has become a disaster machine, churning out civil wars, starvation and environmental crises with depressing regularity. Turning off the disaster machine will require not only that we respond to humanitarian emergencies, but that we also act preventively, to address the silent crisis of underdevelopment - of chronic and growing poverty, of mounting population pressures and of widespread environmental deterioration - which underlie these tragic events. The lessons of Grameen can help provide some guideposts for that effort. All of us who are making the journey owe a great deal to the staff and members of Grameen for helping to light the way, and to Susan Holcombe for making this experience more accessible to those who wish to follow.

James Gustave Speth
Administrator
United Nations Development Programme
New York
January 1995

Focusing on Implementation

Development practitioners persist in the search for models of poverty alleviation. Does the single intervention of targeted credit work best? Or do we need multiple interventions in order to create sustainable improvements in the lives of poor people? The quest for a good model is driven by the need for efficient use of scarce resources for poverty alleviation.

But are we in the development community looking in the wrong direction? Is it the model that is so important? The experience of Third World non-governmental organizations (NGOs) - for example Grameen Bank and BRAC in Bangladesh - tells us that very different models have been remarkably successful in ameliorating poverty. The search for models, or magic solutions, may distract us from how models are implemented.

Poverty alleviation may not depend on a model or blueprint but on a management process. Grameen Bank, BRAC and other NGOs are management systems for exercising leadership and for organizing and implementing action for poverty alleviation. Good models can only be as good as their implementation is effective. Implementation, when well-managed, can adapt and improve models on the basis of experience.

1

INTRODUCTION

...we shall never understand the complex reality of organizations if we persist in studying them from a distance. We learn how birds fly by studying them one at a time, not by scanning flocks of them on a radar screen.[1]

There is a broad consensus in the development community about the priority of poverty alleviation and also about the importance of participation and empowerment. In the search for models or even magic solutions to poverty, the significance of participation and empowerment to the implementation of models is often overlooked. Participation and empowerment are essentially functions of process, not models. They occur only because of processes set in motion by the staff of organizations implementing poverty alleviation. To make participation and empowerment of the poor possible - whatever we think those concepts mean - we need to enable the participation and empowerment of those staff working directly with poor people. For how can staff who feel disempowered and excluded from participation be expected to encourage the participation and empowerment of poor people?

This book is for development practitioners. It turns away from the search for theories and models of how poverty alleviation works. It argues instead that we need to be concerned with the process of managing poverty alleviation that makes a lasting difference to the lives of poor people. It starts by observing field managers of a poverty alleviation organization in Bangladesh (Grameen Bank), one at a time, as they perform their daily work. From observation of the reality of individual field staff, it moves to general statements about process.

How does Grameen Bank manage a staff of more than 14,000 who make daily visits to groups of village borrowers, often trudging miles through rain and mud? Why do Grameen staff maintain a reputation for high performance and honesty when most other extension services fail in their mission of reaching the poor? To find the answers we need to watch how Grameen Bank workers perform, one by one. Starting with Grameen's field staff and their achievements, this book works backward and tries to map out how Grameen Bank managed its poverty

1

alleviation efforts, and in what ways that management can be called participatory and empowering.[2]

The aim is not to develop a new model of poverty alleviation. Models may be misleading when there is so much variety in human responses to poverty. What works in one situation may fail in the next. We need a process that allows the emergence of models suited to the specific circumstances of poor people. We need management guidelines that allow participatory and empowering poverty alleviation to take place.

The nature of management at Grameen bears resemblance to the strategic quality movement in private or corporate sector management. Grameen's management style contrasts with traditional models of managing development assistance and where aid delivery has been a one way process. At its core, Grameen is based on a set of values. Principally there is the assumption that people, whether staff or clients, have the capacity to solve problems, to work hard, to be honest. People are resources to be supported and enabled, not potential problems. Grameen senior management fosters staff participation and empowerment within a framework of shared vision and values. Grameen goes further, devolving responsibility and authority not only to field staff but also to clients. Field staff and clients have responsibility and authority for the basic work of lending and collecting savings and repayments. Senior management can decentralize decision-making on basic work because Grameen has a strong vision or purpose, widely understood and shared by staff and clients.

Grameen invests heavily in inculcating its vision and in maintaining its organizational culture. Management has designed a range of mostly positive motivational devices to assure honest performance in a milieu where corruption is common. It uses its management information systems not only to generate information for decision-making and performance control up the ladder, but also to disseminate information back to lower level staff so they can control their own performance. We can begin to understand the complex reality of a poverty alleviation organization when we examine specific organizations at close range.

Poverty and Development

Grassroots organizations and alternative development advocates are to a large degree responsible for directing our current attention to the poverty question. Their advocacy has sharpened our perceptions of the severity and incidence of persistent poverty. They documented the adverse impact on the poorest of the structural adjustment policies of the 1980s. They argued that the enormous development investments of post World War II period not only failed to transform the situation of the poorest, but may even have exacerbated poverty.

Major international development and finance institutions now also give renewed priority to poverty alleviation. The World Bank focused its 1990 **World Development Report** on poverty. The United Nations Development Programme (UNDP) has identified poverty alleviation as part of its quest for a new paradigm of sustainable human development. The debate continues over whether development assistance has increased or decreased the extent of poverty. The established financial institution view is that large sections of the poor in the developing world have experienced economic progress and that without development assistance the situation of the poor would have been worse.[3]

Poverty alleviation, however, is difficult to define. Even more difficult is measuring whether and to what degree poverty alleviation has occurred.[4] What unites most definitions of poverty alleviation is broad agreement that "participation" and "empowerment" of clients are essential to poverty alleviation. This book argues that development projects can never expect to achieve participatory and empowering poverty alleviation unless the management of those projects is itself participatory and empowering. Intervening organizations must model the participatory and empowering behaviors that they expect clients to adopt. Development practitioners who call for participation and empowerment need to practice what they preach!

Many years ago David Korten suggested that the development community needed to move away from rigid models and focus on the implementation process. Specifically he called for a "learning process approach" that allows implementation to adapt to experience. Rigid models, he suggested, are not very useful when we know so little about how rural development or rural poverty alleviation actually occur.[5] It is because we lack models of poverty alleviation that some development management specialists urge attention to managing implementation, and away from elaborate planning.[6]

Yet planning has been the most powerful tool among the armaments of the development profession. The post World War II era of planned development assistance has been dominated by economists and the tools

3

Introduction

of economic analysis. Major financial institutions like the World Bank have structured development thinking with a search for economic models and a reliance on an input-output approach. Though the World Bank is moving to program and sector lending, and other large agencies follow suit with a program approach, organizational structure (centralized) and professional culture (that of economics) orient these institutions toward the planning phases and away from implementation and management.[7] The banking process, for example, is concerned with planning and loan appraisal. It invests heavily in developing models for implementation - models that they believe are replicable - and in preparing for appraisal. Once the appraisal is complete, there is little incentive to become involved in implementation, except to ensure that funds are spent according to plans.

What many of these efforts share is scant attention to the process of implementation. The planning tools of major financial institutions are undeniably powerful, but, as Paul Streeten implies below, we should not accept uncritically the models of the financial institutions.

...the large international financial institutions exercise a monopoly of power and wisdom, and propagate at times prematurely crystallized orthodoxies.[8]

Without involvement in implementation and its management, the large institutions lose the opportunity to test and season their orthodoxies.

Using the Lens of Management

Asking questions about participation and empowerment in the management of poverty alleviation organizations is the entry point for exploring how intermediary organizations successfully manage poverty alleviation. If participation and empowerment are an essential part of poverty alleviation, must poverty alleviation organizations themselves have a participatory and empowering style of management? Asking the question invites examination of how successful organizations manage poverty alleviation. Exploring the question requires defining whether and in what ways the management is participatory and empowering, and to what extent this is responsible for outcomes. One intended result is to produce a specific description of how the staff of one organization - successful at poverty alleviation - manage. The other is

4

to generate process guidelines for managing poverty alleviation that may be relevant in other cultural and economic settings.

To explore participatory and empowering management in one organization committed to poverty alleviation required identifying a suitable subject for study. Selection criteria included organizational commitment to poverty alleviation that encompassed participation and empowerment of the poor; evidence that the interventions of the organization had resulted in poverty alleviation, including participation and empowerment, for its intended clients; and a size and scope of work that would make findings relevant to a discussion of medium to large scale poverty alleviation interventions.

Grameen Bank in Bangladesh met the criteria (see Chapter 3 for discussion of the Bank) and agreed to the proposed research. Grameen is a poverty alleviation organization, registered as a bank, that in 1991 was making loans to more than one million very poor rural individuals. (By 1994 the total number of borrowers has reached nearly two million.) Its outreach surpasses that of many government departments. There is empirical evidence of Grameen Bank's positive impact on the income and assets of its clients, as well as on indicators of participation and empowerment that suggest that Grameen clients are beginning to take direction of their own lives. The international development community recognizes its record of extending loans, of achieving repayment rates in excess of 98 percent, and of generating savings among growing numbers of poor Bangladeshis.

Grameen also illustrates some of the apparent paradoxes inherent in our definitions and uses of the concepts of participation and empowerment. Supporters of Grameen Bank praise it for participatory management and operations that empower staff. Detractors argue that it is hierarchical, dependent on the leadership of its founding manager, and that its work is highly regimented, not participatory and empowering. Studying Grameen is an opportunity to examine the relationships among strong leadership, accountability, participation and empowerment.

Participation and empowerment are emotionally evocative ideals. Most people respond positively to the ideals of participation and empowerment, and to the notion of management and of organizations that are participatory and empowering. Our folk wisdom calls for consistency between words and deeds. Some management and motivation theorists have proposed that workers will respond with greater productivity when their jobs and responsibilities are enlarged and when they have a chance to find fulfilment in work. Nonetheless management research on real organizations shows that not all members of organizations want to participate and be empowered. Many are quite happy with repetitive work requiring no responsibility.

Some management theorists also argue for consistency between an organization's goals and values and the ways in which it behaves; between its "espoused" and its "actual" vision and values. This would imply that an organization seeking to achieve participation and empowerment for its clients would have itself to be participatory and empowering.

There is a management literature that addresses issues of participatory management, industrial democracy, and empowering management. There is also a development management literature concerned with the how of organizing and managing poverty alleviation and development. The best of the latter is oriented toward community management. Some deals with government departments and non-government organizations (NGOs). Only a little of it marries development experience with the social science research on organization and management. This book draws on existing management concepts to analyze the practice of Grameen Bank.

The methodology used in this research, described more fully in an Appendix, relies heavily on Henry Mintzberg's approach to observing what managers actually do, as opposed to what they say that they do. Mintzberg believed that most studies of the work of managers were really descriptions of what managers **ought** to be doing, not what they do. In 1973 he observed five North American managers for five days each, carefully recording and classifying the actions of managers. The research for this book observed six Grameen Bank field managers for four to six days each. Bouncing along on the back of a motorcycle or bicycle over Bangladesh roads, sharing meals, or attending group meetings, a research assistant and I observed, recorded and coded the work of the managers. Other research methods used include focus groups discussions, interviews and review of documentation.

Though an inductive approach seeks to avoid preconceptions, this book does have a bias. It starts with the premise that participation and empowerment, in some form, are for most people desirable ends. This is not to deny the importance of efficiency and effectiveness as criteria in poverty alleviation work. Grameen was chosen for study because of its demonstrated effectiveness. The concepts of participation and empowerment are the filter through which the management practices of Grameen Bank are assessed. The scope of observation and other research was largely limited to major conceptual areas which the management and organization literature (see Chapter 2) have suggested are relevant to participation and empowerment. These include:

- vision and values of the organization
- inculcation and maintenance of vision and values
- structuring of work
- decision-making
- planning and control.

The categories above represent preconceived notions, albeit notions grounded in the literature, about how participation and empowerment are evidenced in management and organization. The open-ended research techniques produced evidence about the nature of participation and empowerment in a poverty alleviation organization.

Readers of this book may have interest in specific aspects of poverty alleviation or Grameen Bank. The book can and should be read selectively. Chapters 2 and 3 are introductory to the presentation of findings. Chapter 2 is directed to academics as well as practitioners. It addresses the basic questions of identifying and defining the key concepts of poverty alleviation, management, participation and empowerment. It draws on a partial review of literature from the fields of management and organization; development economics; development management; and poverty alleviation.

Chapter 3 may be particularly interesting to the generalist who wants a description of how Grameen operates. Its purpose is to provide justification for the choice of Grameen Bank as the focus of a case study. To do so it provides evidence of other researchers on Grameen Bank's impact on the income, assets, participation and empowerment of poor people and on the commercial viability of the Bank. Chapter 3 describes Grameen's model of poverty alleviation through targeted rural credit. It also includes background information on Grameen Bank as it is organized for implementation of poverty alleviation.

Chapter 4 describes how Grameen leaders manage organization vision and values, finding that

- Control of vision and values is highly centralized;
- The Grameen vision of poverty alleviation encompasses both income/asset changes as well as empowerment and participation of

the identified target group of poor;
■ The stated values of Grameen are empowering of staff work and participation in poverty alleviation work;
■ Operating level staff and managers espouse the same vision and values as the central leadership.

Chapter 5 explores the consistency between the espoused values of Grameen Bank and those values in practice by looking, in particular, at evidence on the management behavior of field level managers, and assessing that evidence in the context of the surrounding societal culture. There is a tension between the values of the surrounding society and those of Grameen Bank. Grameen is in effect attempting a culture change for its employees. The consistency between espoused values and managers' actual behavior appears to be reinforced by the structuring of work and informal routines.

Chapter 6 examines the role of central leadership in managing organizational vision and values. It is really about how to motivate a large extension staff. It finds that

■ Senior management makes motivation and maintenance of staff morale a key priority.
■ Management relies on a range of techniques - induction training, rapid promotion, and formal and informal communication systems - to build and sustain motivation of field staff.
■ In the absence of real monetary rewards, management taps needs for recognition, status, belonging to a distinctive organization; pride in accomplishments; and an altruistic commitment to service in sustaining motivation.

Chapter 7 explores the nature of participation and empowerment in the structuring of Grameen Bank work by looking at the design of decision-making on a key operation - approval of the loan. It also looks at the design of jobs at the operating level.

■ Operational decision-making on lending in Grameen is decentralized to the level of operations management. Participation in the decision process as well as in responsibility for assuring implementation of the decision is diffused throughout the operating level, even to the extent of involving clients in ways that makes traditional organizational boundaries permeable.[9]

- The design of jobs at the field or operating manager level empowers and engages participation of those managers within the framework of organizational objectives and the fixed flow of work.
  - Jobs of field managers are not highly specialized, but are enlarged and enriched horizontally and vertically.
  - Job design is neither highly formalized nor highly organic. Planning and reporting requirements establish the direction and pace of work. Tradition, if not detailed job descriptions, suggest without mandating, common patterns for work task design. Within that framework and the structure of plans and regular reporting requirements, there is latitude for field level managers to design their own tasks. The organizational culture encourages initiatives.

The way in which an organization plans and coordinates its work or output is seen as an indicator of its centralization or decentralization, or the degree to which it empowers staff lower in the hierarchy. The management literature describes planning and control systems as a continuum moving from decentralization to centralization. Performance control allows decentralization while action planning is centralizing. Grameen Bank relies on a performance control system to regulate and control performance in the operating core. Chapter 8 explores the operation of the performance control system in Grameen Bank to identify the ways in which it is decentralized, participatory and empowering.

- Grameen planning targets are first set at the operating level and then aggregated as they move up the hierarchy.
- Grameen manages the tension between the need for overall organizational viability with the need for responsiveness to the client by using a range of indicators.
  - The priority given to performance indicators varies by levels in the organization.
  - Operating level managers give priority to performance indicators that track the viability of their unit's activities with clients.
  - Senior management gives priority to indicators tracking the overall performance of the organization.

Grameen's information system tracks quantitative data on a wide range of performance indicators used in the credit operation and returns this data in a timely fashion to the operating managers responsible for action. An informal information system supplements the formal system, confirming or invalidating quantitative performance data and providing a context for analysis.

Chapter 9 draws the preceding chapters together and explores the overall hypothesis that poverty alleviation organizations committed to the empowerment and participation of the poor can organize and manage work in ways that are both centralizing and decentralizing. Control of vision and values is highly centralized. They provide the framework within which decentralization, participation and empowerment take place. Organization leadership maintains tight central control of the values and vision of the organization through management of the organization culture and using a variety of motivational tools. The vision focuses performance on clear and simple tasks of the basic work of the organization. The values are centered on people and on the capacities of people, both clients and staff, to perform to agreed standards. Central control of vision and values, and of accountability for serving organization vision and values, is the framework for participation and empowerment. It takes individual performance seriously. The practical manifestation of staff participation and empowerment can be found in the decentralization of key operational decisions to the lowest possible level, the involvement of staff in the development of work plans and performance goals, the encouragement of staff initiative in non-routine work and of staff suggestions for maintaining and re-shaping organization vision and routine procedures.

Notes

1. Henry Mintzberg, **The Nature of Managerial Work** (New York: Harper and Row, 1973), iv.
2. Richard Elmore writes about the "backward mapping" approach in "Backward Mapping: Implementing Research and Policy Decisions" in Walter Williams, **Studying Implementation: Methodological and Administrative Issues** (Chatham, N.J.: Chatham House Publishers, Inc., 1982).
3. World Bank, **World Development Report**, (Oxford: Oxford University Press 1990), 1-6; Robert Cassen and Associates, **Does Aid**

Work?   Report to an Intergovernmental Task Force (Oxford: Clarendon Press 1987), 298.   Interestingly, the largest national decrease in numbers of people living in poverty occurred in China between 1978 and 1985 where the estimated total fell from 270 million to 90 million persons.

4. See, for example, Paul Streeten, "Poverty Concepts and Measurement", **The Bangladesh Development Studies** 18 (September 1990). Chapter 2 discusses some of the issues involved in defining poverty and its alleviation.

5. David C. Korten, "Community Organization and Rural Development: A Learning Process Approach" **Public Administration Review** 40 (September/October 1980).

6. Dennis Rondinelli makes this point on the basis of his analysis of World Bank and UNDP projects.   Dennis Rondinelli, **Development Projects as Policy Experiments: An Adaptive Approach to Development Administration** (New York: Methuen, 1983): 74-79.

7. Crane and Finkle explore the constraints of organizational structure and professional culture in their study of the World Bank: Barbara B. Crane and Jason L. Finkle, "Organizational Impediments to Development Assistance: The World Bank's Population Program", **World Politics**, 33 (July 1981), 516-533.

8.   Paul Streeten, "Poverty Concepts and Measurement", **The Bangladesh Development Studies** 18 (September 1990), 18.

9. Traditional bureaucratic theory places clients outside the organization. Open systems theories acknowledge that clients are an important variable in the organizational environment and that many organizations, like universities and hospitals, may incorporate clients in the performance of some organization functions. Grameen Bank is a special case where clients perform core organizational tasks of monitoring and accountability.

2

POVERTY ALLEVIATION, PARTICIPATION, EMPOWERMENT AND MANAGEMENT

...what we know, or think we know, enters into our theories, models and policies.[1]

Poverty alleviation, participation and empowerment are powerful words. They evoke a positive response in most of us. Development practitioners and donor organizations are no different. From the Percy Amendment tacked on to a foreign aid bill by the U.S. Congress to the recent spate of international donor reports on poverty that highlight participation and empowerment, donors have long espoused a commitment to serving "the poorest of the poor", to alleviating poverty.

What do these words mean - poverty alleviation, participation and empowerment? Do development practitioners and donor organizations know what they mean? And, more to the point, do they know how to translate these concepts into practical programs that produce results?

This chapter describes the range of definitions of poverty alleviation, participation and empowerment and suggests how these concepts relate to management ideas and practice. The succeeding chapters will look through the lens of these ideas and practices in an effort to discover whether and in what ways Grameen Bank management is participatory and empowering.

Seeking Definition

Trying to define what we mean by poverty alleviation, participation and empowerment is problematic. There is a large and growing literature on poverty alleviation, participation and empowerment, multiplying the range and nuance of definitions. The literature cuts across disciplines, including economics, anthropology, sociology, politics and geography.

It traverses political-economic philosophies, from Marxist to capitalist interpretations of the distribution of wealth and power.

There appear to be dichotomies among some of the definitions. Participation and empowerment are seen as being ends, or as being means. Poverty alleviation action is seen as originating at the grassroots or at the policy level. The focus of some on process may seem in opposition to the emphasis of others on planning. The distinctions among definitions of poverty alleviation, participation and empowerment often reflect professional, institutional and philosophical biases. In reality, there is considerable overlap among the definitions. Participation and empowerment are both means and ends. There needs to be a synergy between the policy environment and grassroots action. Planning sets directions and mobilizes resources, but it needs to be influenced by wide participation and moderated by the lessons of implementation experience. The problem is not one of choosing from opposing definitions and viewpoints, but of achieving a balance among them.

Two Dimensions of Poverty Alleviation

Broadly speaking development scholars and practitioners acknowledge two dimensions of poverty: the income or asset dimension and the more fluid power and participation dimension. In a report on poverty in Bangladesh, the North-South Institute gave one definition which attempted to encompass both dimensions:

> Poverty is a state of economic, social and psychological deprivation occurring among people or countries lacking sufficient ownership, control or access to resources to maintain acceptable living standards.[2]

These dimensions are articulated and measured differently. The income/asset dimension seems largely concrete, objective and susceptible to measurement. The participation and empowerment dimension seems subjective and difficult to measure. Nonetheless, the two dimensions are interdependent.

The income and asset dimension of poverty at first seems to be easy to define and measure. Institutions are daily defining poverty in a myriad of programs. Governments construct poverty lines using income levels and estimates of what it costs to maintain the minimum standard of living. Organizations like Grameen Bank use landlessness to define the poor and determine eligibility for loans. The United Nations Children's Fund uses the under five mortality rate as one broad index of lack of a basic asset, health. The United Nations Development Programme (UNDP) is constructing a human development index which measures assets by educational attainment, health status and purchasing power.

These real life measures reflect the range of efforts to capture the full impact of poverty. Simple money income does not reflect changes in prices of goods and services required, nor does it get at the proportion of people living in poverty; the degree of the poverty; and the distribution of the poverty among classes and ethnic groups and within households. There has been a movement toward more complex measures which take into account multiple facets of poverty, as with the Physical Quality of Life Index (PQLI) and the more recent UNDP Human Development Index.[3]

Streeten's 1990 article summarizes the thinking that has been done on defining and measuring poverty. He argues that being able to monitor success in poverty alleviation is important, particularly when that success results from government, donor or other interventions. We need to know, he suggests, the changes in the number of poor people; the severity of their poverty; the length of time they are in poverty; and the changes in access to the physical inputs (calories, housing, hospitals, schools) and to capacity building resources (literacy, good health); and in distribution patterns among groups in society and within the family.[4]

Streeten seems to make the link between the asset and the empowerment dimensions of poverty alleviation when he talks about non-material benefits. On his list are good working conditions, the freedom to choose jobs and livelihoods, self-determination, the assertion of traditional and religious values, empowerment or access to power, the opportunity to join and participate actively. The poor, he says, may value these more than an increase in material benefits. "These are all important objectives, valued both in their own right and as means to satisfying and productive work." Streeten acknowledges the difficulty of measuring these aspects, but warns of falling victim "to the twin fallacies that only what can be counted counts, and that any figure, however unreliable, is better than none."[5]

Defining Participation and Empowerment

Definitions of participation and empowerment, as implied in discussion below, cannot be separated from values. At this point there are two issues to note. First there is widespread acknowledgement of the importance of participation to the success of poverty alleviation programs. Many argue that this commitment of the development community may be more rhetoric than reality. Development agencies from the World Bank to grassroots non-governmental organizations (NGOs) verbalize their commitment to participation; less often do they state the steps necessary to structure operations that allow participation beyond that of voluntary labor in projects designed by outsiders. Second, the importance of participation as an element in development emerges from perceptions of failed development efforts.

In his 1980 article calling for an adaptive implementation process, Korten noted not only the size of the world's poor, but also the likelihood that the poorest did not benefit from and may even have suffered loss as a result of development. He called for new approaches "to bring the poor more rapidly into full participation in development decisions, implementation and benefits."[6] Over the past thirty years or more there has been an effort to find a solution to poverty in the developing world. Strategies of community development, integrated rural development and basic needs followed one another through the 1950s, 1960s and 1970s. Participation evolved in the 1970s as a response to inadequacies of previous strategies and continues to be a "major issue" in development thinking.

If the literature on identifying and measuring the concrete aspects of poverty is long and inconclusive, the material on the participation and empowerment dimensions is even more complex. Participation and its practice in poverty alleviation in the developing world is a large and separate subject with its own literature. It is probably not possible to give a definition of participation which is comprehensive and commonly accepted. Participation has been appropriated by all schools in the development community. Oakley notes that "it is almost now reactionary seriously to propose a development strategy which is not participatory...".[7] Tendler attempted to capture the range of meaning imputed to participation. On one level, participation may consist of voluntary labor by the recipients, with decision-making remaining top down. At the other end of the spectrum there is genuine representative or grassroots participation of the poor in the identification, design and management of the intervention. In between are variations such as decentralization of decision-making to representatives of local elites.[8]

Oakley identifies three manifestations of participation: contributions by target groups to pre-determined projects; organizations, structured and supported either by development workers or by the people themselves; and empowerment through, for example, acquisition of new management, negotiation or decision-making skills.

In some cases, empowerment refers to control over resources. Overholt and colleagues, writing about gender issues in development, talk about access to and control over resources and benefits.[9] Korten also defines empowerment as control, "specifically the control over and the ability to manage productive resources" and that "...control over an action should rest with the people who will bear its consequences." He links control to accountability, and he adds a generative definition to the usual distributive understanding of power. Effectively, he argues that empowerment need not be a zero sum game where the poor gain at the expense of another class.[10]

Amartya Sen has developed the concept of entitlement, implying recognized or de facto rights to an equitable share of the resources of society.[11] In other cases, power is linked to organization or the lack of it. The poor can be exploited because they are fragmented and unorganized. By organizing themselves, they can begin to redress the imbalance in the rural power structure and, in so doing, gain access to and control over the resources of the society.[12] Another element is that of being on the inside, of participating. Being empowered is "... owning the capacity to act, rather than be acted on."[13]

The distinction between acting and being acted upon echoes the writing of Paolo Freire. To Freire, being human is to be a "Subject", with capacity to think and act; "Objects" are thought about and acted upon. The oppression of the poor is ended when both the oppressed and their oppressors are transformed or liberated through dialogue and consciousness raising. During this process people come to understand the causality of poverty. Out of this understanding new relationships are established where both sides are equals, or "Subjects". The implication for poverty alleviation is that development is something which cannot be done to or for a person, but must be done with them.[14] True poverty alleviation involves participation both of the poor and of the larger society.

Key words which emerge from these definitions are access, control, entitlement, deciding, acting, awareness, and participation. Participation is seen as an essential ingredient of empowerment. To be empowered means that you are participating. To participate in turn modifies the nature of the access, control, deciding aspects of empowerment. In a world of finite resources, everyone cannot control everything. Participation introduces the possibility of equity into distribution. Participation is also an ingredient of the acting and consciousness raising aspects of empowerment definitions. To participate is to act, to be a "Subject". Oakley sees this awareness as basic to sustaining participation. People move from a passive acceptance of their situation to a critical understanding which allows them to structure their own reality.[15]

Finally, participation and empowerment are linked like a hand and glove. They are different, but they depend on each other to give meaning and purpose. Participation represents action, or being part of an action such as the decision-making process. Empowerment represents sharing control, the entitlement and the ability to participate, to influence decisions, as on the allocation of resources.

Participation and Empowerment: Means or Ends?

As suggested above, participation and empowerment are each seen variously as a means or an end. This is a simplistic dichotomy, but it reveals useful distinctions. Participation and empowerment are ways to harness the human resource component of any development undertaking, contributing to the effectiveness, efficiency and sustainability of an activity. The World Bank notes that successful projects have usually involved the poor at the design and implementation stages.[16] Arguments for participation and empowerment of the poor (through skills training and access to inputs) include:

- better information for project design; feedback for project adjustment;
- adaptation of programs to local conditions;
  ' ability to tap local technical knowledge and resources;
- more efficient use of existing government services and improved access for the poor;
- better cooperation of intended beneficiaries.[17]

Group formation, involving the participation of the poor, can be seen as a means and/or an end. Groups may be seen only as a mechanism to receive inputs, or their mobilization may support the expressed goal of a project to create the cohesion, trust and solidarity necessary for sustained group action.[18]

Participation and empowerment are for perhaps the majority of us deeply held values or goals. As noted earlier, for Freire and others, participation and empowerment are the transformed state we should be seeking, where the oppressor and the oppressed meet each other on new and equal ground. Others, for example dependency theorists, argue that poverty is more than a psychological state and is rooted in economic and social structures. There can be no poverty alleviation without fundamental structural changes in the internal politics and economies of countries, and in the world economy.

The implications of this structural perspective are profound. It is at the heart of the problem major donors face when they try to engage in poverty alleviation work. Their partners are necessarily governments. But governments, because of the political, social and economic systems they represent, are part of the problem. They may be sustained by the systems that disempower the poor. Grameen itself, we shall see, faces real or potential threats from power structures. It may not be possible to sustain participation and empowerment at the grassroots if the structures at the sub-national and national levels do not evolve to support increasing participation and empowerment of the poor people.

Poverty Alleviation: Top Down or Bottom Up?

Institutions today scarcely dare espouse a top down approach to development or poverty alleviation. David Korten has likened the top down approach to "delivered development" and a bottom up approach to "participatory development". In fact, these two approaches may not be dichotomous; under ideal circumstances, they are complementary. What the implied dichotomy reflects are the institutional differences in approach to poverty alleviation. Though everyone pays lip service to bottom up approaches,[19] the interpretation varies by the nature of the institution. On the one hand, development, poverty alleviation, and empowerment are something which people do for themselves. On the other hand, policies and projects develop and empower people. The intervening agency plays the decisive role.

18

If policies and projects empower people, then the focus of action will be on the policy level. If people empower themselves, then the focus of change efforts is where the people are, at the village or community level. The policy versus grassroots level approach may reflect differences in institutional origins and structures. The larger financial institutions are creatures of governments.[20] Their staff relate to government leadership, not to grassroots people. Their core technologies are planning, policy analysis and project appraisal. They rely on a centrally controlled project approach, which specifies inputs to be delivered for expected outputs within a set time period. They also focus on shaping the policy environment. The World Bank in its 1990 document on poverty noted that "attacking poverty is not primarily a task for narrowly focused anti-poverty projects...it is a task for economic policy in the large." Its recommendations revolve around two policy elements: incentives which promote productive use of labor of the poor; and provision of basic social services.[21]

Grassroots organizations, in contrast, focus not on policy but on change for individuals and groups, one by one. Grameen Bank takes banking services to the village. Core technologies include process approaches, education and group formation. The Bangladesh Rural Advancement Committee (BRAC) begins with promoting the formation of Village Committees. Inputs arise out of the group.

Also linked to the top down - bottom up and the policy versus grassroots dichotomies is the debate in development circles over the project versus process approaches to development or poverty alleviation. The project approach, shaped by the discipline of economics and the tools of policy analysis, provides a logical framework for transforming inputs into desired outputs. The project document has been useful for the large financial institutions as the basis of legal agreement between the donor and the recipient government. Projects were the building blocks or "cutting edge of development";[22] "...the project approach has endured as a disciplined and systematic approach to analyzing and managing the use of development resources in order to achieve important development objectives".[23]

By the late 1970s, scholars and practitioners with considerable experience in rural development began articulating reservations about the capacity of rational planning and the project approach to "blueprint" a development intervention. They called for an adaptive process. The project approach served the control and accountability needs of donors and governments, but not the needs of the poor.[24] Rondinelli, who

19

based his conclusions on a study of UNDP and World Bank projects, noted the frequency with which projects had to change course in the middle of implementation. In many cases the original design was faulty in that it was unable to predict and control for all the problems of implementation. Development projects operate under conditions of uncertainty. Project design needs to provide the capacity for adaptability during implementation. Implementation needs to be able to detect and learn from errors and to seize opportunities.[25]

This book focuses on one facilitator organization, Grameen Bank, that seeks to produce poverty alleviation. The term facilitator does not come from management specialists, but from development professionals. Facilitator organizations or people are the "missing links" who are "neither villagers or policy makers but nevertheless serve an essential organizational function by facilitating reciprocally helpful interactions between the two groups."[26] Interest in facilitator organizations coincides with the emergence of interest in participation and empowerment in the mid-1970s. Korten in his 1980 article noted the need for donor organizations to reorient themselves. He pointed to structural and accountability factors that orient large donors to projects which are large, capital intensive and non-participatory. He cited the need for organizations "with a capacity for embracing error, learning with the people, and building new knowledge and institutional capacity through action".[27]

Practitioners and researchers have begun to look at the management and organization of facilitator organizations, drawing to some extent on management concepts. Esman and Uphoff began by looking at institution building concepts in rural development.[28] A number of North American practitioner-scholars called for "bureaucratic reorientation" or restructuring of donor organizations to facilitate participation.[29] Some work has been done on the management of major donor supported projects. These include case studies describing the process approach of successful poverty alleviation interventions[30] and analysis of the experience of government departments.[31] Little has been written about the organization and management of the donor organizations themselves.

Curiously, the discipline of public administration has contributed little to an understanding of **managing** development and change. The brand of public administration exported to the developing world particularly in the 1950s and 1960s was divorced from the growth taking place in management thinking in the United States and elsewhere. It was tool oriented and predicated on an assumption that the transfer of administrative systems would overcome obstacles to development. It made a sharp distinction between administration, which was to be scientific and value neutral, and policy, where issues of values and leadership entered in.[32]

The contribution of public administration to development has begun to change. Public administration practitioners and scholars have an opportunity to bridge the gap between development practice and new ideas emerging in other disciplines, especially business management and strategic quality management.

Building Participation and Empowerment

Participation and empowerment do not just happen. There has to be a strategy and a set of actions to allow them to develop.

What do we mean when we say that an organization has a participatory or empowering management style? From the range of definitions above, one can suggest that participation and empowerment are degrees on a continuum. The greatest degree of participation and empowerment may exist when operating staff are seen as the **starting point for action**, and as the **source of skills and capacities**. Participation and empowerment thrive when staff become the Subjects and the decision-makers. Decisions and planning emerge from those who are closest to the action; and responsibility is given and accountability demanded from staff. There is also a **psychological** element to participation and empowerment; that of an achievement of a sense of worth by being on the inside and by taking responsibility.

Moving the poverty alleviation concepts of participation and empowerment to the management arena is difficult and it suggests possible paradoxes. What does it mean, for example, to suggest that a staff member makes or participates in organizational decisions. Does a junior staff person really have the opportunity to express ideas and contribute suggestions that help shape organization action?[33] With the exception of a limited number of small, truly egalitarian, organizations, formal power rests with senior management in an organization. They may choose to share power in a participatory organization. They still retain veto power. Charles Perrow noted:

The veto is important; it is like saying we have a democratic system of government in which people elect their leaders. Workers and managers can have their say, make suggestions, and present arguments, and there is no doubt this is extremely desirable. It presumably results in the superior making better decisions - but they are still his decisions.[34]

Elsewhere Perrow suggests that these boundaries or premise controls could even be called "brainwashing", "manipulation" or "false consciousness".[35] The potential veto power of the organization may appear to put boundaries on the empowerment of staff to participate in the decision process.

In the organizational setting, there are indeed boundaries within which participation and empowerment can take place. Senior management in an organization can shape the environment within which participatory and empowering management takes place. Senior management or leaders in an organization can limit the choices (and reduce the risks) by establishing the goals or vision of an organization, and by working to assure that goals are shared throughout an organization. They may achieve and maintain this commitment as a result of leaders' actions, capitalizing on human needs for involvement and identification with a group, or by manipulation of rewards and sanctions.

Likewise the psychological aspects of participation and empowerment in an organization - the self-awareness that is central to the thinking of Freire and others - are bounded by the scope of the organization. A participatory and empowering poverty alleviation organization would be expected to encourage or affirm in staff a sense of their own value as agents of change. It would tend to create an environment where staff feel themselves empowered, not only to be part of a worthy enterprise whose goals they share, but also to contribute to achieving those goals. Empowered staff are staff who feel free, even encouraged, to take initiatives in solving problems and achieving goals.

Many management consultants and organization development specialists see participatory and empowering management as a means to higher morale and to unleashing the creative potential of staff. They also see empowering management as generative, expanding rather than just redistributing the power in an organization.[36] The quality management movement is grounded in assumptions that the experience and creativity of workers are underutilized assets, and that quality control is most efficiently achieved through participation of the work

force and through maximum delegation.[37]   Others point out that we
can value empowerment and participation as ends in themselves.

The next subsections describe the major concepts used to explore
the management of Grameen Bank and suggest how these concepts
relate to participation and empowerment.

Vision and Goals

The vision or goals of an organization are important. Vision provides
the direction in which an organization is going and can serve as the
standard to which the performance or production is regulated.
Clarifying and communicating organization vision or mission has long
been seen as a critical management function. Barnard noted in the late
1930s that the "inculcation of belief in the real existence of a common
purpose is an essential executive function."[38] While Barnard appeared
to suggest that the executive wins that commitment from staff, others
have pointed to a top down reality where senior management has the
power to "structure the subordinate's environment and perceptions in
such a way he or she sees the proper things and in the proper light."[39]

Whether inculcating vision facilitates a participatory process or is
itself a manipulative process, shared vision does provide boundaries
within which action and decision-making take place.   Whether
managers are successful in inculcating vision has implications for
participatory and empowering management. To the extent that vision
is stable and shared, staff will themselves decide or behave in ac-
cordance with the limits of that vision. The sharing of vision creates
the conditions for autonomy and participation.

Part of vision is a clear understanding of the basic or core work of
the organization and of who the customers are. Thompson's call for
managers to "buffer the technical core" assumes that managers have no
trouble identifying what the technical core or basic work of the
organization is, and who their customers are.[40] Managers have the
task of defining and communicating vision. Without common vision
and common understanding of it, decision-makers at all levels of the
organization "will pull in different directions without being aware of
their divergencies".[41]

Language and communication skills are central to developing
common commitment. It is not enough to have a powerful vision.
Managers need to be able to communicate vision and values, and to stir

others to accept them. This is particularly important when the organization is attempting to introduce change, and is asking staff to undertake unconventional or difficult work, or to adopt new behaviors. Pondy noted that "The real power of Martin Luther King was not only that he had a dream, but that he could describe it, that it became public, and therefore accessible to millions of people".[42]

Values and Culture

The values or culture of an organization are often linked to discussions of vision. If vision tells where you are going, values or culture describe how you go about getting there. Value systems in an organization affect perceptions of authority and subordination, status, collaboration, social distance, change and innovation. Together the values structure the culture of an organization.

Edgar Schein defined organization culture as

...a pattern of basic assumptions - invented, discovered or developed by a given group as it learns to cope with its problems of external adaptation and internal integration - that has worked well enough to be considered valid and, therefore, to be taught to new members as the correct way to perceive, think and feel in relation to those problems.[43]

Culture can have immense, usually tacit, impact on employee behavior inside an organization. Behavior in an organization strongly influences motivation. Maintaining (or changing) culture is a managerial activity.[44]

Culture or assumptions are reflected in management behavior or style of behavior. Managers can value subordinates as resources waiting to be mobilized to produce, or as inputs that need to be controlled and supervised. Peters saw the role of the manager as unlocking the potential of staff. He prescribed manager/leader behaviors he saw necessary to empowering staff. These include "compulsive listening"; "cherishing the people at the front"; "delegating 'authority' in a way that truly empowers"; and "vigorous and visible pursuit of bureaucracy bashing".[45]

Others have suggest that participatory and empowering management style are only sometimes appropriate. Kenneth Blanchard proposed four types of leadership styles, each appropriate to different levels of staff skills and commitment. Where staff are highly committed and competent, a managers needs only to support them. Where staff have low skills and low motivation, managers need to be directive and controlling.[46]

Motivation

Motivation is linked to vision and values. It is that force or drive that pushes, impels individuals to work to achieve certain ends. Motivation is a concept with roots in the discipline of psychology. Motivation has many definitions. A basic definition suggests that motivation is derived from the satisfaction of human needs at different levels. The first level of needs is physiological or survival; others are safety, love, esteem, and self-actualization (or fulfillment of one's potentials). Once needs at one level are filled, humans will want to satisfy those at the next level.[47]

Another definition assumes that individuals decide (or are motivated) to make an effort on rational grounds. In this view, motivation is a function of the expected reward for behavior or performance, the value placed on the reward, and the expected capacity to achieve the goals set for the individual's work.[48]

Related to this concept of being motivated by the expectation of reward is the dichotomy between extrinsic and intrinsic rewards. Valued rewards, like salary increases, are seen as a common form of extrinsic motivation. But motivation may have intrinsic components that include variety, challenge or significance of the work; responsibility for results; and knowledge of results. Indeed, it may be high performance in a job that gives satisfaction (rewards) rather than expectation of rewards that produces high performance.[49]

In an organization that encourages the empowerment and participation of staff to undertake poverty alleviation work, one would expect intrinsic factors to be important in explaining the motivation and commitment of staff.

Structure

Structure is not used here in the traditional sense of organization charts and the formal structure of positions and power. Structuring is an active process. Managers have a number of tools to shape the ways in which work is done in an organization. This book focuses on four mechanisms: job design, training and indoctrination systems, decision-making systems and planning and control systems. In defining variables to be analyzed, this research relies heavily on the conceptual framework developed by Mintzberg in **The Structuring of Organizations.**[50] In what ways do the explicit efforts of senior management to structure the work of the organization serve to expand or contract the autonomy and participation of operating staff?

Design of Positions
Job specification is a way of limiting discretion or autonomy of staff in an organization, and of assuring standardization and consistency. It can be done by detailed specification of the steps in each job or for each type of work, or through organizational rules. When the work or tasks are highly formalized, power passes from the worker to the person who designs the rules or specifications.

Bureaucratic structures, where behavior is standardized or formalized, work well in stable environments. Organic structures, characterized by the absence of standardization or behavior formalization, operate better in changing environments where innovation and adaptation are required.[51] In other words, if workers must solve problems, capitalize on opportunities, deal with uncertainty, it may be counterproductive to prescribe their work behavior. If staff work is routine and an objective is consistency and fairness (as with bank customers), then it is productive for the organization to specify, formalize or standardize work behavior. Autonomy, discretion, and capacity to innovate may be associated with empowerment. There may also be practical reasons of efficiency that call for allowing autonomy in conditions of uncertainty. But staff may not always seek participation and empowerment.[52]

Training and Indoctrination
Training and indoctrination can also influence the design of positions. Training develops skills and knowledge while indoctrination inculcates the norms of the organization. Professional skills training may reduce the need for rules or formalization in the organization as the standards are inherent in the training. Inculcation of vision and values is a way of socializing staff to the organization's culture. Because culture pro-

vides a set of norms for behavior, inculcation of the organization culture also lessens the need for close supervision or job specification.

One function of culture is to serve as a "religion" or "ideology" which builds a common approach on "How to manage the unmanageable and explain the unexplainable". Ideology may reflect the goals or ideals of the organization and motivate or fortify staff during difficult periods. It may reduce anxiety about uncertainty. Culture inculcated may also develop in staff a common language, group solidarity, a sense of inclusion which sustains commitment to organization goals.[53] It may also produce that sense of being on the inside, of being empowered to work for change, that affirms for staff their own value. As suggested earlier, the inculcation of culture may be manipulative.

Decision-making Systems
Control means influence or "say" in actions or decisions. When we talk about decision-making, what is really important is the action that results, and who has a say or influence on that action. Decisions are not simply the choice of a course of action. Decisions are a process that begins with the identification or recognition of the need to decide. Devolution of decision-making power down the hierarchy or to specialists outside the line is a transfer of power away from senior management. Vertical decentralization transfers power to managers lower in the line. Horizontal decentralization distributes power among people at the same level or among a group with technical responsibility. Decentralization and centralization are a continuum. Control of all steps in the decision-making process is the tightest form of centralization. Control or influence over one or more steps in the process (e.g. the identification of problems for decisions and the development of alternatives) moves the organization toward decentralization.

Horizontal decentralization is associated in the management literature with organizational democracy or participatory management. Participation is a value prized by many for its intrinsic worth. Proponents argue that participation may contribute to increased efficiency and productivity, though research findings on this assertion are mixed.[54] Organizations with influential rank and file staff can be as effective as organizations where the staff are not influential. Research does suggest that organizations in which both management and workers are influential will be more effective than those where neither have much influence.[55]

Planning and Control Systems
The function of planning and control systems is to assure that outputs correspond to standards or expectations. There are two fundamentally different types of planning and control systems. Performance control focuses on overall performance and relies on after the fact monitoring of results. Action planning seeks to specify the specific activities to be done to produce outputs. Planning and control systems can be categorized in terms of hierarchy. Performance control is both a bottom up and top down, as well as a sometimes iterative, process. Overall objectives are set at the top, perhaps with input from the bottom. Units at the bottom propose their own performance standards, negotiate them with higher levels, and have autonomy in deciding how to achieve them. Action planning, in contrast, is primarily top down, with the center establishing strategic plans, programs, and ultimately the schedules and operating specifications that lead to outputs.[56]

There are linkages and hybrid versions of these two different approaches to planning and control. Conceptually they present a range. Performance planning could be called a more participatory and empowering approach. It involves lower staff in setting of goals and allows autonomy in deciding what actions to take to meet the goals.

Other Conceptual Issues

Can Western concepts of management be applied in an analysis of management of poverty alleviation in a non-Western setting? And if they can, how should they be adjusted for the differences in national culture and in the dominant bureaucratic culture of the country?

Mendoza suggests that Japanese or Southeast Asian models of management, based on a different system of values, may be more appropriate in the developing world than the models of the West.[57] In the same book, Siffin argues that the organization and management models that the United States has been exporting through its development assistance programs are based on Weber's ideal and geared to strengthening the central machineries of government. The U.S. was exporting public administration, not management. It was exporting outdated thinking, not emerging models which might better have served development needs.[58]

To some extent the question of the usefulness of Western management concepts may not be whether, but which. Human relations and culture schools of management address some of the issues of shared vision, teamwork, and group cohesion which are said to be central to Asian models of management. A few scholars, from East and West, have begun to apply new management and organization concepts to development implementation.[59]

National culture becomes an important variable when it reinforces or conflicts with the poverty organization's culture or attempts to create culture. Where there is inconsistency, it can create dissonance and conflict for staff, and can impede the inculcation of culture and the behaviours it sanctions. Abecassis writes about aspects of culture in relationship to development in Bangladesh. He speaks of the strength of fatalism or "karma" among rural people. One is poor because Allah willed it. The implication is that little can be done to change fate. Social classification and hierarchy determine relations at the village level. A patron-client relationship is unequal. For the poor it contributes to an identity marked by powerlessness and worthlessness.[60] The norms and assumptions governing the lives of rural Bangladeshis are a specific manifestation of the general state of powerlessness and exclusion from participation.

The prevailing bureaucratic culture in Bangladesh is rooted in the national culture. Huque notes the pervasive centralizing tendencies of government. Both the colonial and independence governments attempted to maintain control of rural areas by creating local institutions they could dominate. Where strong local leaders emerge, they are leaders of the rural elite and are unwilling to decentralize power to lower levels.[61]

The staff of a poverty alleviation organization come from the larger society. In the case of Grameen Bank, many staff were born and raised in rural areas. Out of 38 Area Managers questioned, 27 had grown up in rural areas. To some degree they may carry the norms and assumptions of their childhood into their work culture. They may have embraced new norms and assumptions about human behavior during their university experience, but not necessarily converted these espoused values into practice. And they may not be aware of discrepancies between what they believe and what they do. The existence of discrepancies gives opportunity for conflict with the empowerment and participation goals of the organization.

Conclusion

The focus of this book is participatory and empowering management in poverty alleviation. Structural variables - delegated decision-making, performance control systems and organic job designs that are vertically and horizontally enlarged - contribute to decentralization and an empowering and participatory management. Further, the capacity to decentralize, and therefore to allow participatory and empowering management, is dependent on strong central control of organizational vision and values and central creation and maintenance of an organization culture that supports that vision and values. This includes central management of induction or indoctrination into organizational values and vision and maintenance of commitment to those values and vision.

Figure 1.   Variables in Participatory and Empowering Management

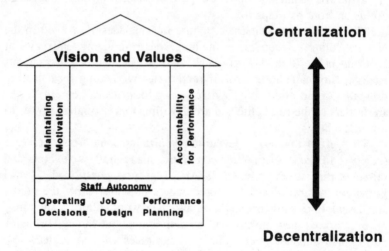

Figure 1, which is derived from the Grameen Bank logo, is intended to represent these relationships. The roof of the house provides the umbrella under which all activities take place. The vision and values, maintained by senior management, specify what will take place under the shelter of the house. The operating staff are the foundation. They exercise autonomy on basic operating decisions, design of operating work and setting and meeting performance goals - all within the shelter of organizational vision and values. What binds the house together are the pillars of motivation, centrally maintained, and accountability for performance goals, which is decentralized.

We may envision participatory and empowering management as being at one end of a continuum, but that image may not be very helpful if we are uncertain how to measure participation and empowerment on that continuum. Figure 1 is an attempt to picture the dynamics of participatory and empowering management at the operating core, and the influence of centralizing and decentralizing forces. Like any model, that in Figure 1 is simplistic. The text in Chapters 4 to 8 will attempt to provide the detail and the nuances.

Notes

1. Paul Streeten, "Poverty Concepts and Measurement"; **The Bangladesh Development Studies** 18 (September 1990) 18.
2. North-South Institute, **Rural Poverty in Bangladesh, A Report to the Like-Minded Group** (Ottawa: North-South Institute, 1985), i.
3. See, for example, UNDP, **Human Development Report 1993** (New York: Oxford University Press, 1993).
4. Paul Streeten, **op. cit.**, 1-18.
5. **Ibid**, 14.
6. David C. Korten, "Community Organization and Rural Development: A Learning Process Approach", **Public Administration Review** 40 (September/October 1980), 480.
7. Peter Oakley, **Projects with People: The Practice of Participation in Rural Development** (Geneva: International Labour Organization, 1991), 6.
8. Judith Tendler, "What Ever Happened to Poverty Alleviation" (New York: Ford Foundation, 1987).
9. Catherine Overholt, Mary Anderson, Kathleen Cloud and James Austen, **Gender Roles in Development Projects** (Hartford: Kumarian Press, 1985).
10. David C. Korten, **Community Management: Asian Experience**

and Perspectives (West Hartford: Kumarian Press, 1986), xix, 6.
11. Amartya Sen, **Poverty and Famines: An Essay on Entitlement and Deprivation** (Oxford: Oxford University Press, 1981).
12. In reporting on his research on extension services in Kenya, David Leonard notes the "squawk factor"; those who complain or are likely to complain (effectively) are more likely to receive extension services. Later he suggests that one of the conditions for effective extension is that clients have political power. David K. Leonard, **Reaching the Peasant Farmer: Organization Theory and Practice in Kenya** (Chicago: University of Chicago Press, 1977), 188-190; 249. See also Michael Lipton on the poor and organization: Michel Lipton, "Why the Poor Stay Poor", in John Harris, ea., **Rural Development** (London: Hutchinson University Library, 1982).
13. Theodore Thomas, "Reorienting Bureaucratic Performance: A Social Learning Approach to Development Action" in Juan-Claude Garcia Zamor, **Public Participation in Development Planning and Management: Cases From Africa and Asia** (Boulder, Colo.: Westview Press, 1985), 19-20.
14. Paolo Freire, **Education for Critical Consciousness** (Cambridge: Center for the Study of Development and Social Change, 1973), 1-43.
15. Oakley, **op. cit.**, 195.
16. World Bank, **World Development Report 1990** (Oxford: Oxford University Press, 1990), 4.
17. Oakley, **op.cit.**, 14-18.
18. **Ibid**, 184-186.
19. Barber Conable, then World Bank President, urged that "...development must be more bottom up, less top down". World Bank, **Sub-Saharan African, From Crisis to Sustainable Growth** (Washington: World Bank, 1989), xii.
20. Barbara B. Crane and Jason L. Finkle describe the institutional and historical factors which re-enforce centralization and a top down approach at the World Bank, in "Organizational Impediments to Development Assistance: The World Bank's Population Program", **World Politics**, 33 (July 1981), 516-533.
21. World Bank, **op. cit.**, 17.
22. J. Price Gittinger, **Economic Analysis of Agricultural Projects** (Baltimore: Johns Hopkins Press, 1972), 2.
23. Warren Baum and Stokes M. Tolbert, **Investing in Development: Lessons of the World Bank Experience** (Oxford: Oxford University Press, 1985), 5-6.

24. Korten was one of the first to use the term "blueprint" to describe the tight, highly planned project approach, to which he proposed an alternative, "learning process approach". See also Dennis Rondinelli, **Development Projects as Policy Experiments: An Adaptive Approach to Development Administration** (New York: Methuen, 1983). Rondinelli refers to the critiques of policy analysis written by Charles Lindblom and Aaron Wildavsky at this period.

25. **Ibid**, 14, 74.

26. Bruce F. Johnson and William C. Clark, **Redesigning Rural Development: A Strategic Perspective** (Baltimore: Johns Hopkins University Press, 1982).

27. Korten, **op. cit.**, 480.

28. Milton J. Esman and Norman T. Uphoff, **Local Organizations: Intermediaries in Rural Development** (Ithaca: Cornell University Press, 1974).

29. See Garcia Zamor, **op. cit.**

30. Korten, **op. cit.**

31. For example, Leonard, **op. cit.**

32. See William Siffin, "Two Decades of Public Administration in Developing Countries", Francis Sutton, "American Foundations and Public Management in Developing Countries", in Joseph E. Black, James S. Coleman and Laurence D. Stifel, eds., **Education and Training for Public Sector Management in the Developing Countries** (New York: Rockefeller Foundation, 1976), 49-60, 117-133.

33. See Douglas McGregor, **Leadership and Motivation**, Essays of Douglas McGregor edited by Warren G. Bennis and Edgar H. Schein (Cambridge: The M.I.T. Press, 1966), 59-60.

34. Quoted in Henry Mintzberg, **The Structuring of Organizations** (Englewood Cliffs, N.J.: Prentice-Hall, 1979), 204.

35. Charles Perrow, **Complex Organizations: A Critical Essay** (New York: Random House, 1986), 130.

36. See Tom Peters, **Thriving on Chaos: Handbook for Management Revolution** (New York: Harper and Row, 1987); Rosabeth Moss Kanter, "Power Failure in Management Circuits", in Jay M. Shafritz and J. Steven Ott, **Classics of Organization Theory** (Chicago: Dorsey Press, 1987).

37. See, for example, J.M. Juran, **Juran on Leadership for Quality: An Executive Handbook** (New York: The Free Press, Macmillan, Inc., 1989), 264, 291.

38. Chester Barnard, **The Functions of the Executive** (Cambridge:

Harvard University Press, 1968), 233.

39. Perrow, **op. cit.**, 127.

40. Thompson used the term "buffering the technical core" to describe a key function of managers. This assumes that managers at the operating levels know what the core work is. See James D. Thompson, **Organizations in Action** (New York: McGraw Hill, 1967). Peter Drucker called it knowing "what our business is and what it should be", implying a forward looking vision. See Peter Drucker, **Management: Tasks, Responsibilities, Practices** (New York: Harper and Row, 1985), 77.

41. Drucker, **op. cit.**, 77.

42. Louis R. Pondy, "Leadership is a Language Game", in Harold J. Leavitt, Louis R. Pondy and David M. Boje, eds., **Readings in Managerial Psychology** (Chicago: University of Chicago Press, 1989), 230.

43. Edgar H. Schein, **Organizational Culture and Leadership** (San Francisco: Jossey-Bass Publishers, 1989), 9.

44. Chris Argyris and Donald Schon, **Organizational Learning: A Theory of Action Perspective** (Reading, M.A.: Addison Wesley, 1978), 230.

45. Tom Peters, **op. cit.**, 468.

46. Kenneth Blanchard, "Situational Leadership II", brochure prepared by Blanchard Training and Development, Inc., Escondido, California, 1985.

47. A.H. Maslow, "A Theory of Human Motivation" in Leavitt et al., eds., **op. cit.**, 20-35.

48. David A. Nadler and Edward E. Lawler, "Motivation: A Diagnostic Approach", in Leavitt et al., eds., **op. cit.**, 3-19.

49. Perrow, **op. cit.**, 87.

50. Mintzberg identified nine design patterns that can be controlled by a manager: job specification, behavior formalization, training and indoctrination, unit groupings, unit size, planning and control systems, liaison devices, vertical decentralization and horizontal decentralization.

51. Mintzberg, **op. cit.**, 81-94.

52. Mintzberg notes the findings of Crozier that "...workers with a strong need for security and with low tolerance for ambiguity prefer jobs that are highly formalized as well as highly specialized". (**Ibid**, 91.) This implies a resistance to being empowered, and a willingness to remain, in Freire's terms, Objects rather than Subjects.

53. Schein, **op. cit.**, 65-84.

54. Mintzberg, **op. cit.**, 184-208.
55. See Perrow, **op. cit.**, 113.
56. Mintzberg, **op. cit.**, 148-160.
57. Gabino A. Mendoza, "The Transferability of Western Management Concepts and Programs, an Asian Perspective", in Black at al., eds., **op. cit.**, 63-67.
58. Siffin, "Two Decades of Public Administration", in Black et al., eds., **op. cit.**, 151-156.
59. See Leonard, **op. cit.**; Jan R. Moris, "The Transferability of Western Management Concepts and Programs, an East African Perspective", in Black et al., eds., **op. cit.**; Norman Uphoff, "Activating Community Capacity for Water Management", in Korten, **op. cit.**; and Atiur Rahman, "Participative Management Style of Grameen Bank", a paper presented at a workshop on Grameen Bank jointly organized by the Bangladesh Bank Training Academy and the Bangladesh Institute of Bank Management, Dhaka, 27 January 1987.
60. David Abecassis, **Identity, Islam and Human Development in Rural Bangladesh** (Dhaka: The University Press Limited, 1990), 34-40; 62-69. See also the discussion in Chapter 5.
61. Ahmed Shafiqul Huque, **Politics and Administration in Bangladesh: Problems and Participation** (Dhaka: University Press Limited, 1988), 168-170.

3

GRAMEEN BANK

In South Asia, Bangladesh is gaining a reputation as the most innovative and receptive nation in making use of grass-roots organizations, like the rural Grameen Bank movement, which give support to village entrepreneurs.[1]

To explore the empowering and participatory aspects of managing poverty alleviation intervention at Grameen Bank, it is useful to have an overview of Grameen operations. What is Grameen Bank, how does it operate, and what impact has it had on the poverty of its intended beneficiaries? This chapter describes Grameen Bank both as a model (rather, several models) of poverty alleviation, and as a management process for implementing the models.[2] It also reviews much of the available evidence on Grameen's impact, and establishes the basis for an assumption of this study that Grameen Bank has been successful. Preparatory to those tasks, this chapter offers basic data on the Bangladesh setting in which Grameen functions and on Grameen Bank itself.

Bangladesh: The Socio-economic Setting

Bangladesh is one of the world's least developed countries by any standard measure. The World Bank estimated per capita income at $170 in 1988, with an annual growth rate of 0.4% between 1965 and 1988. Estimates of the extent of poverty in the country suggest that 70% or more of the population live below the poverty line. For many, survival is the daily challenge. Agriculture is the primary sector, but most of the poor are landless. Data show that landlessness has been growing in the last decade. Women are heavily represented among the poor and landless. Opportunities are limited. An estimated 25-30% of the labor force is not productively employed. Low wages, shortage of capital and a low level of skills and literacy contribute to low productivity. The Government has not had capacity to play a leading role in development and is handicapped by a highly centralized mode of operation and constricted resources.

Since 1970, Bangladesh has seen a remarkable emergence of national non-governmental organizations contributing effectively to participatory, grassroots development. Development efforts of all kinds are constantly threatened by natural and political disasters. Sitting at the head of the Bay of Bengal, the nearly sea-level expanses of Bangladesh are subject to the regular ravages of cyclone and flood. Political events, for example the 1991 influx of 250,000 Moslem refugees from neighboring Myanmar, destabilize development planning and financing. Chapter 5 discusses briefly the basic features of Bangladesh culture and the interaction of culture and development.

Scope of Grameen Bank Operations

Grameen is both a Bank and a poverty alleviation organization. The creation of the Bank came after seven years of experimentation with an action research project intended to demonstrate that the poor can generate enough income from small enterprises to support small scale lending. Grameen became a government registered bank in 1983 with the objective of providing credit to the rural poor. In 1990 the Grameen Bank ordinance was changed, effectively moving control from the Government, which previously appointed a majority of members of the Board of Directors, to elected borrower-members who were given nine out of twelve seats on the Board of Directors.

Grameen Bank is a large organization - the largest non-governmental organization operating in Bangladesh. In 1991 Grameen Bank operated 808 branches in 19,984 villages of Bangladesh, serving more than 884,000 members. (By May 1994, Grameen Bank had 1,915,000 members in 34,243 villages served by 1,042 Bank branches.) If one assumes that the benefits of savings and credit reach the whole family of 5 to 6 people, then the beneficiary population increases to around five million persons out of a total rural population of about 97 million (early 1991).

At the end of 1990, Grameen Bank had a total of 13,626 staff members. Of these only 583 were employed in the Head Office; the remainder were engaged in field work. A total of 7,133 were employed in 9 Zones in direct banking activities. The others were employed in technical projects such as Deep Tube Wells, fish and shrimp farms or as trainees.

At the time of the research, cumulative general and collective loan disbursement amounted to Tk. 78,185 lakh or US$ 223,400,000, of which $6,500,000 was disbursed in the preceding month. (By May 1994, cumulative loan disbursement exceeded US$1 billion, of which US$26.2 million were disbursed in May of that year. Total savings, including the Group Fund, were US$ 80.1 million.) Additionally, the Bank disburses housing and technology loans to members. Total loan disbursement in 1990 was annually about US$100,000,000. Total Group Fund and Emergency Fund savings mobilized from members amounted to Tk. 7,992 lakh or US$22.8 million in early 1991. Grameen calculated the percentage of loans overdue (unrepaid after two years) at 1.32%; those unrepaid at one year were 3.49% of the total amount.

The Grameen Model

Grameen Bank is best known as an operating model of targeted, small scale rural credit.[3] Grameen is also a model of an experimental, learning organization. While its present experimental activities are not the focus of this research, it is important to establish that innovation and experimentation are continuous. Grameen is structured in a way that buffers the established credit activities from the uncertainties of new technologies and enterprises being tested by other units of the Bank.

Grameen's basic model of small scale credit has been fixed in its essentials since the mid-1980s. The methods of group organization and group collateral for lending were established through years of experimentation following from the initial effort in Jobra village in 1976. The model of targeted rural credit is now so sufficiently tested that it has been expanded horizontally at a rapid rate since 1983. The horizontal expansion is modular; new branches, areas and zones are opened following the established pattern. One long-time observer of Grameen compares its expansion pattern to that of MacDonalds' franchises.[4] It is the management and organization of this basic lending and savings operation that is the focus of this study.

Targeted Rural Credit

The Grameen model of targeted rural credit is simple. A basic assumption of the Grameen model is that the very poor in rural areas already have the skills, but not the small amount of capital, required to operate a viable productive enterprise. Existing banks are biased to the rich and literate and are institutionally based. If banking operations are taken to the people and small scale capital (average $60 - 70) is made available, poor men and women will use it. By organizing the borrowers into groups of five that are responsible for the loans of each of the members and by requiring weekly instead of annual repayments, Grameen management can assure a low default rate. Weekly savings in a Group and an Emergency Fund are a mandatory feature of Grameen membership. The organization of up to six groups into a center develops group leadership skills and capacity to demand entitlements from Government departments and rural leadership and to undertake self-help activities. The model of Grameen targeted rural credit is represented in Figure 2.

Figure 2. Grameen Bank Credit Model

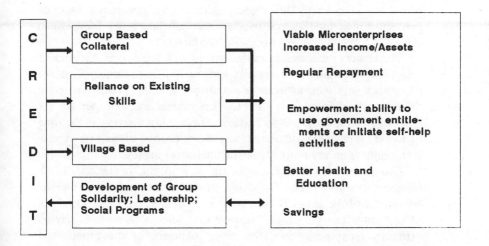

Grameen Bank

The characteristic of the Grameen model of poverty alleviation that distinguishes it from most other organizations is that awareness building, consciousness-raising, and leadership development follow rather than precede the delivery of credit services. Grameen field operations focus on forming groups and initiating the loan process. The time from when a like-minded group of five men or five women decide to join together until they are recognized as a group may take only a few weeks. Members must first participate in what the Bank calls continuous training, learning Bank rules and regulations and the Sixteen Decisions (see below). Once all the members demonstrate their knowledge of the Bank and the group is recognized, their attendance and participation in weekly center meetings is observed for about a month. Then loans may be extended to two group members. If these two members repay regularly for the next two months, two more members may become borrowers. The chairman of the group is the last borrower of the five. Five percent of each loan is automatically paid into the Group Fund. Members must also make weekly payments of one taka into the Group Fund. This Fund belongs to the group and its use is decided on by the group. Additionally members pay about 25 percent of their total interest payment into an Emergency Fund which serves as life and accident insurance for members.

The centers meet weekly in the village with their Bank Assistant at a regularly scheduled time, usually very early in the morning so as not to conflict with work obligations. Groups sit in the center shelter in their groups of five. In a complete center meeting, one can see six rows of five members neatly seated. The weekly meeting is the time of weekly repayment, deposits to savings accounts, discussion of new loan requests or any other matter of interest to members.

Group and center operations are key to the operation of the Grameen credit model. First the group is the guarantor for the repayment of the loan. If a member is in default, no other members of the group can get loans. In practice, when a member is having difficulty repaying a loan, the other members of the group, and sometimes the center, work out a solution that assures repayment to the Bank. The Bank Assistant may or may not be involved in this problem-solving. Secondly, all business, especially exchange of money and discussion of loans, is carried on openly. This reduces the opportunities for corruption, and increases the opportunities for members to take responsibility.

Each group elects a chair and a secretary. The center elects a chief and a deputy chief. These officers serve for one year and may not be re-elected until all others eligible have had the opportunity to serve in a leadership position.

Social Interventions

Election and rotation of officers in the centers underlines the importance of the non-banking but social and empowerment aspects of the Grameen model. It is only after participating in the group and the center over time that members acquire the self-confidence and skills, or the awareness, to take on other actions. The very existence of an organized group and an organized center creates an institutional opportunity for other interventions. In 1984 a national workshop of 100 women center chiefs agreed to the Sixteen Decisions or resolutions on improved social practices to be implemented by all the members:

Sixteen Decisions

1. The four principles of the Grameen Bank - Discipline, Unity, Courage and Hard Work - we shall follow and advance in all walks of our lives.
2. Prosperity we shall bring to our families.
3. We shall not live in dilapidated houses. We shall repair our houses and work towards constructing new houses at the earliest.
4. We shall grow vegetables all the year round. We shall eat plenty of them and sell the surplus.
5. During the planting seasons, we shall plant as many seedlings as possible.
6. We shall plan to keep our families small. We shall minimize our expenditures. We shall look after our health.
7. We shall educate our children and ensure that they can earn to pay for their education.
8. We shall always keep our children and the environment clean.
9. We shall build and use pit-latrines.
10. We shall drink tube-well water. If it is not available we shall boil water or use alum.
11. We shall not take any dowry in our sons' weddings, neither

> shall we give any dowry in our daughters' weddings. We shall keep the center free from the curse of dowry. We shall not practice child marriage.
>
> 12. We shall not inflict any injustice on anyone, neither shall we allow anyone to do so.
> 13. For higher income we shall collectively undertake bigger investments.
> 14. We shall always be ready to help each other. If anyone is in difficulty, we shall all help them.
> 15. If we come to know of any breach of discipline in any center, we shall all go there and help restore discipline.
> 16. We shall introduce physical exercise in all our centers. We shall take part in all social activities collectively.[5]

Prospective members study the Sixteen Decisions and are tested on them before being accepted as members. Most meetings begin and end with a Center Chief leading members in recitation of some of the Sixteen Decisions. Special social programs, designed by Grameen Bank and sometimes funded by outside donors, encourage or enable members to implement the Sixteen Decisions. Successful implementation of the Decisions will enable members and their families to be healthier, better educated and more productive, creating a stronger base for banking operations. The Decisions represent more a social awareness rather than the political consciousness-raising and mobilization that many non-government organizations believe must precede sustainable development for the very poor.[6]

Scaling-up Microenterprises

Targeted rural credit is only part of Grameen's activity. Grameen also models the learning process approach in its efforts to expand vertically, giving the very poor access to new, productive technologies. Grameen Bank leadership recognizes that microenterprises, particularly of the sort operated by Grameen borrowers, will result in only marginal improvements in the lives of the very poor. The most common use of Grameen credit is for a livestock investment, mostly purchase of a cow for milk, or for fattening and resale. Khalid Shams, the Deputy Managing Director of Grameen, suggested that such micro-scale interventions may move borrowers from just below to just above the poverty line; families will have three meals a day where once they had one; and children may go to school where before they did not.

Management sees the need to break the technology and management barriers that keep poor people from benefitting from more sophisticated and productive technologies. The size of the economy as a whole needs to expand in order to allow more rapid income growth for the poor and the landless. This means a rapid rise in productivity in the agriculture sector, which is the base of the Bangladesh economy.

It was against this background that Grameen Bank set up a Research and Development unit and launched the Studies, Innovation, Development and Experimentation (SIDE) effort with support from the Ford Foundation. SIDE has experimented with new technologies - tillers, threshers, edible oil crushing mills, handloom factories - and with management and ownership systems. Grameen has also taken over management of failed or abandoned Deep Tube Wells (DTWs) (using the support from the UNDP Capital Development Fund), fish ponds and other assets with the intention of finding ways of operating these facilities with collective client/member ownership and management.

This research focuses on the credit and savings operation of Grameen Bank, not on the new experimental activities. Once credit and savings activities were highly experimental. Now they have become standard operations, to which incremental changes may be made. Grameen Bank continues to experiment, but it structures its work so that the innovation is separate from core credit and savings work. In effect, senior management buffers the core work (banking operations) from the uncertainties of research and development work. Referring to the SIDE activities, a donor report noted that "these enterprises are by nature unconventional and untried." By separating them from Grameen Bank's own fund, Grameen Bank is protected "from the high risk of failure in experimental and innovative enterprises."[7]

Organizing to Implement Poverty Alleviation

Implementation is an organizational task. In the Grameen model of targeted credit, Center activities are crucial to the implementation of credit provision. The role of the Center has implications for the way in which the whole organization is designed.

Rather than using an organization chart to map the relationships of various parts of the organization, Figure 3[8] charts the not always hierarchical ways in which work and information flow through the different parts of the organization. At Grameen Bank the core or basic operations are the group formation, center functioning, lending, savings mobilization, collection functions and social mobilization (Sixteen Decisions). Lending is to individuals, but through groups. The groups effectively guarantee the loan. Forming groups of five unrelated people, who link with five other such groups in a Center, becomes a critical function of Bank staff. All basic banking and other activities are carried out through groups and centers by the Bank Assistants, **and by the Bank members or clients**. The clients, by becoming members, actually become a part of the organization as well as the customer. Bank Assistants are supervised by the Branch Bank Managers. Area Managers supervise usually ten Branch Banks in a 100 square kilometer area.

Area Managers perform only a limited number of actual banking functions (loan approvals, group recognitions) but play a significant coordinating and management function. Ideally, in the Grameen organizational design, ten Area Managers report to one Zonal Manager. At the time this research began there were nine Zones in Grameen (there are now eleven). The Zonal Managers are thus at the top of the middle line, reporting to the strategic apex or central management, which in Grameen includes the Managing Director, the Deputy Managing Director and the General Manager.

The strategic apex is responsible for assuring overall functioning of the organization: managing relations with the outside; and managing organizational strategy or vision and values. The strategic apex deals also with Grameen's policy body, its Board of Directors of which nine members are elected by the client/members of the Bank. A secretariat supports the strategic apex, backstops the Board meetings and also the promotion process and facilitates an informal flow of information.

The technostructure at Grameen Bank performs not only the planning, changing, designing and training functions, but also the experimental operations. This part of the organization includes departments in the Head Office for Planning, Monitoring and Evaluation, Training and Special Programs, Research and Development and Technology. Planning is a new function at Grameen. Monitoring and Evaluation manages the formal management information system and has been strengthened by donor support that has allowed, for example, establishment of Zonal monitoring and evaluation units and computerization of Zonal Offices. The training and Special Programs Depart-

Figure 3. Grameen Bank: Major Work and Information Flows and Interactions

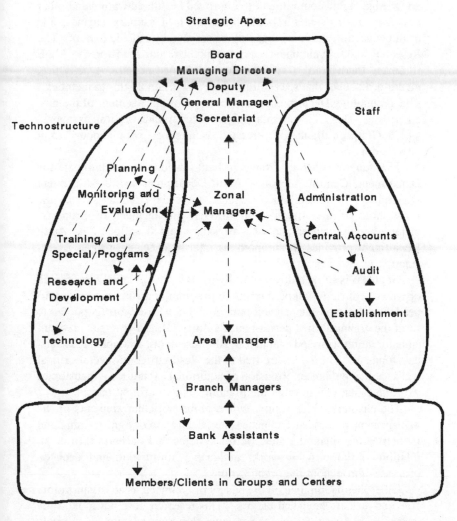

Adapted from framework developed by Mintzburg, <u>Structuring of Organizations</u>

ment manages training and operates three training institutes.

The Special Programmes encompass the variety of social mobilization activities supported through the Branch Banks. These may include the workshops held on a scheduled basis for members to increase knowledge of and commitment to improved health, education and other practices; aid to center schools; installation of sanitary latrines; and health education activities that may be assisted by outside donors. The Research and Development Department is responsible for the SIDE (Studies, Innovation, Development and Experimentation) activities, mentioned above, that seek to introduce new technologies to members. The Technology Department is responsible for management of the new enterprises, Deep Tube Wells (DTWs), fish ponds, shrimp farms, in which Grameen Bank has invested, sometimes with support from outside donors.

The support staff in Grameen Bank include the Administration Department, Central Accounts, Audit Department and Establishment Department. As their labels suggest, these departments service the functioning of the organization through management of property, materials and finances and of staff salary and benefits. The Audit Department provides an autonomous internal check on proper use of resources.

Grameen is broken down into divisions by geographic Zones, each of which replicates others in terms of program and administrative staff needed to manage independent banking units whose work is pooled to form the organizational performance. Zonal Offices have staff responsible for monitoring and evaluation, administration, accounts, and social development. The Zones are tied to the Head Office in several critical ways: policy guidance; provision of additional capital for expansion or working costs; and through the planning and control systems.

The chapters which follow will explore particular elements of the management process at Grameen, specifically job design, training and indoctrination, planning and control systems and decentralization, in relation to the flow of work, authority, information and decision processes throughout the organization.

Other factors impinge on the design of Grameen as an organization. Age and size are key such factors. This research does not look at the organization over time, but the organization that is Grameen can only be understood in terms of its history. The evolving design of the structure is dependent on the design of the credit intervention model. Grameen Bank began as an action research project of a single economics professor from Chittagong University exploring the nature of poverty. With the aid of his students, he expanded the project into Tangail District in the late 1970s and early 1980s. It was during these years that the basic structuring of the Bank evolved. In the beginning the action research project was a highly organic structure, reliant on mutual adjustment among a small staff to coordinate work. With a largely fixed model of lending and saving and a staff in 1991 of more than 14,000 in nearly a thousand locations, Grameen as an organization has become less organic. It is centralized in policy matters but decentralized in operations.

Stakeholders or outside interest groups have had the potential to influence Grameen. The Government and/or political parties in the country as well as rural elites, seeing the growing organizational capacity of Grameen Bank as a threat to their power, carry the potential power to limit Grameen operations. Donors, who provide low cost capital and funding for training, monitoring and evaluation and other programs, may, intentionally or by weight of their assistance, attempt to intervene in internal organization. Grameen has, in fact, rejected donor assistance when it thought that conditional terms offered threatened its autonomy and integrity. Grameen leadership appears to have managed its external environment through a variety of strategies, including maintenance of informal communication links with Government; avoidance of outright confrontation of rural elites and their interests; and reliance on donors sensitive to issues of donor conditionality.

Uncertainty about political relations with other power interests in the country, as well as the possibilities of political instability, the threat of floods, cyclones and other natural disasters to which Bangladesh is prone, are external factors that will always threaten Grameen operations, or those of any other poverty alleviation effort.

Measuring Impact and Success

Grameen Bank is widely regarded as a successful model of poverty alleviation through credit for microenterprises. CBS **Sixty Minutes** broadcast a program on Grameen Bank in March of 1990, showing the changes in borrowers' lives. The Managing Director has addressed parliaments in Europe and the U.S. Congress. The World Bank is using Grameen Bank as a case study in research on Targeted Finance and Enterprise Development. Development planners seek to replicate the Grameen model.

At the same time there are doubters. Economist Melanie S. Tammen suggests that Grameen's success is overstated, using the criterion that costs cannot be recovered on a sustainable basis. "Grameen Bank itself is not self-sustaining, but heavily dependent on foreign aid." She goes on to suggest that accessible credit is not the answer to poverty, but reform in property rights, limited liability and easy licensing.[9]

Chowdhury and others ask whether the microenterprises funded by Grameen capital have the capacity to sustain themselves and to expand. Most enterprises are low technology (eg. cow fattening or milking) for which the rate of return is limited. "Gradually repeated loans for the same small-scale business can saturate the local market and reduce profits unless the general purchasing power of the people can be increased."[10] This is an issue of graduating borrowers from tiny to larger enterprises, effectively expanding the economy.

Grameen attracts casual criticism from the skeptical and the cynical. Some development practitioners have asked whether the high repayment rates for which Grameen gains praise are won at the cost of excessive pressures on poor people who reduce essential household expenditure to meet weekly payments. Some have suggested that Grameen is promoting a fascist culture with its emphasis on physical exercises at Center meetings, the Grameen salute, and shouted slogans. Grameen's Managing Director Mohammad Yunus responds to these criticisms by referring to practices among the Rotary Club, the Shriners or Japanese workers. "They don't look funny because they do it in five star hotels...Japanese workers shout slogans and do exercises before they start their work, but if Grameen Bank members are seen doing it, it is militarism, Hitlerism."[11]

Impact on the Target Group

What is success? Success at poverty alleviation interventions would seem to be an increase in income and assets as well as increase in empowerment. Proving that success occurred is difficult. This section will cite the evidence available from other evaluations on the impact of Grameen's targeted rural intervention on income, assets, member ability to withstand disasters, on rural wage structure, and on the status of women in the family. The last is used as measure of empowerment, particularly for the more than 90 percent of members who are women. This section will also summarize the evidence on the Grameen's experience in reaching the intended target population and on profitability and sustainability of Grameen's credit operations.

1. Impact on Income and Assets

Mahabub Hossain, a Bangladeshi economist who has done the two principal evaluations of Grameen Bank, notes the methodological problems of determining the economic effects of rural credit programs, particularly in the absence of benchmark data.[12] Hossain collected information on target and non-target families in five Grameen villages and two control villages, including non-participating, target families in the Grameen villages.

Hossain's findings suggest that Grameen Bank loans have resulted in significant increases in member income and assets. Survey data show that Grameen Bank households had incomes that were 43% higher than target group households in control villages and 28% higher than those of non-participants in Grameen villages. The biggest increases in income over non-participating households came in non-agricultural pursuits, particularly processing and manufacturing, trading and transport operations. The income increase was greatest for the absolutely landless and for the marginal landowners. A characteristic of those who took credit, particularly the women, was that they generated new production or employment.

Hossain suggests that the most direct effect of Grameen credit has been the accumulation of capital by the poor. His survey found large increases in the amount of working capital (at a rate of 64% per year, adjusted for inflation, for 975 borrowers with average membership of 2.25 years). Initially borrowers' investment was largely in non-agricultural and agricultural production. After three years borrowers tended to put their money in social investment, housing, education and sanitation. Increases in cattle ownership by borrowers are another indicator of capital accumulation. Before borrowing, 63% of members owned no cattle. At the time of the survey only 44.5% of members owned no cattle, and larger percentages of borrowers owned two or more cows than prior to membership.[13]

Member assets have also been expanded significantly through improved house ownership facilitated by Grameen Bank loans. By the end of 1990 Grameen had extended US$28.9 million in housing loans.

All housing loans go to women. A 1989 evaluation, mandated by United Nations Development Programme assistance to the Grameen Rural Housing Programme, pointed out that housing is not only a social investment but a site for production, processing and storage, thereby contributing to increased productivity.[14]

2. Ability to Withstand Disasters.

Bangladesh is prone to natural disasters that destroy assets and depress productive capacity. In 1991 damage resulting from a cyclone killed more than 100,000 people and caused an unestimated amount of damage. A series of floods in 1987 damaged houses, roads, fields and other facilities. A 1988 flood is thought to have been more devastating, covering two thirds of the country with water for several days and destroying an estimated 1.2 million homes and damaging 2.4 million others. Droughts in 1979, 1981, 1982 and 1989 lowered production levels. The very poor, already on the edge of survival, are most at risk in time of disaster.

Following the 1987 and 1988 floods, Atiur Rahman, an economist from the Bangladesh Institute for Development Studies, surveyed a small number of rural villagers, representing nearly equivalent numbers of Grameen Bank members and a control group in two flood affected areas (75 and 140 each). He sought to explore the capacities of the rural poor to survive and re-establish themselves following natural disaster. He found that Grameen members were less likely to take informal credit from local money lenders and more likely to use working capital from their business or to use their own savings to survive the disaster than was likely in the case of control group members.[15] The conclusion was that Grameen members were protected from impoverishing debt by the assets they had accumulated as a result of credit supported businesses.

3. Impact on Rural Wage Structure.

Daily agricultural labor is a principal source of income for the very poor in Bangladesh.[16] Labor is generally in excess supply in rural markets. Traditionally wage labor is a buyers' market, with the landless poor being obliged to accept whatever wage is offered. An increase in daily agricultural labor rates might be an indicator of two impacts of Grameen Bank (and other NGO activity) in a locality. First, as organized groups rather than individuals, the landless may be able to negotiate better wage rates. Secondly, daily wage rates could rise in response to a decreased supply of agricultural labor because of the engagement of the rural poor in non-farm, credit financed, activities. There is only anecdotal evidence that this has happened, suggesting that average daily wage rates have increased by 30 - 60 percent in areas of high NGO activity.[17]

4. Increased Status of Women Members of Grameen Bank.

Changes in the status of women because of Grameen Bank membership can be seen in measurable economic terms and less easily defined social terms. Key economic measures of women's changed status are their participation in the work force and their increased income and assets. In Hossain's survey of 534 women members of Grameen Bank, he found that 50 percent were unemployed before joining the Bank, while only 21 percent called themselves unemployed after joining. Nearly one third of female members who had previously engaged only in unpaid household work took up paid work.[18] Grameen households also had a higher number of female workers per household than did those in non-participating target groups, and female members reported an increase of 12 days per month of employment as a result of Grameen Bank membership.[19] Female members also reported a higher increase in working capital as a result of membership than did male members, reflecting the bigger change in women's situation.[20]

The most visible sign of women's status may be their ownership of the house and the land on which it sits. The Grameen requirement is that both land and house must be in the name of the woman borrower. The Managing Director has cited this as an incentive for the husband to stay with the family, and the asset, rather than to walk out.[21] The 1989 evaluation of the Housing Programme saw housing as contributing to women's status: "The fact that the housing loan is given in the name of the female head of household or female member of a household, and that it ensures her legal ownership of land and the house, her status is definitely improved. She is now a confident person".[22]

Safilios-Rothschild suggests that the biggest changes that may occur are in men's attitudes toward women and women's attitudes about themselves. Women's participation in groups for borrowing gives them the confidence and support that enables them to assert their rights to economic assets.[23] Mahbub Ahmed, in semi-structured interviews with 120 female borrowers in three districts, found evidence of increased social status of women. The women reported that husbands were more likely to treat them as equals, and that there was a decrease in physical violence, threat of physical violence and other verbal abuse.[24]

5. Reaching the Target Group.

Hossain's 1985 survey of 975 borrowers indicates that Grameen Bank loans went primarily to target group households. Only 4.2 percent of borrowers held 0.5 or more acres of land.[25] There is no evidence suggesting that the bulk of Grameen loans did not reach the target group. The Managing Director acknowledges that the Bank may not always reach the very poorest, the bottom ten percent, but suggests that they are reaching the middle of those (estimated at 70 percent of the population) who are below the poverty line.[26]

Profitability of Grameen Credit

Profitability will remain an issue because it relates to the commercial viability of the Bank and its sustainability. The way one approaches this issue is partly a question of values. Must a Bank seeking to make credit accessible to poor people meet the same standards of commercial viability as a profit-seeking institution?

Tammen has argued that Grameen is not self-supporting and should therefore not be used as a model for poverty alleviation. (Reflecting a different economic and political perspective, she prefers Hernando de Soto's prescription of structural reforms as the most effective antidote to poverty.) She argues that Grameen is able to break even only because of the substantial subsidies it has received from its principal donors. Using Hossain's figures, she notes that the implicit subsidy to borrowers is 39 percent based on the actual cost of funds, or 51 percent if you use the opportunity cost.[27]

Jackelen and Rhyne concur that Grameen is not a profitable bank, but they offer a somewhat different analysis, and perspective. They point out that the current interest rate (1990) of 16 percent is insufficient to cover "the cost of funds (6 - 10 percent) available in Bangladesh plus the overheads (14 percent per annum) and a margin for loan losses or profit." Grameen is able to subsidize loans because donors advance capital, at low cost (2 - 3 percent), prior to disbursement, allowing Grameen to earn interest in the interval. They go on to say

While Grameen's management recognizes that its clients could in fact pay the real cost of credit, it sees itself in the role of transferring benefits from donors to the most disadvantaged sectors of the society. The proof of this transfer can be seen in equating the forced savings generated (which as noted above means a higher effective rate of interest to the borrowers) which is currently in excess of $6 million per annum to an estimate of the donor subsidy. While the latter is difficult to calculate, a rough approximation of 6% on loans outstanding plus half of interest income on deposits for 1990 would total over $5 million as an annual operating subsidy provided by donors. Given that the forced savings generated through lending operations constitutes a tangible asset owned by the clients of Grameen, it would appear that a case for donor subsidy converted as transfer payment could be made.

They also claim that Grameen is the "least subsidized...and most commercial bank" in Bangladesh where institutional credit has only a 30 percent recovery rate in rural areas and less than 10 percent in urban areas.[28]

The question of profitability will remain because of issues of sustainability and the relationship between profitability and scale of lending. Though they use it as a model case, Jackelen and Rhyne suggest that Grameen has yet to be put to the final test. They are optimistic that financial self-sufficiency can be achieved.[29]

Key Features of Grameen Bank

It is not possible to paint a complete picture of an organization in a short space. There are key features of Grameen Bank that are relevant throughout the chapters which follow. Some of these feature distinguish Grameen from other NGOs involved in poverty alleviation in Bangladesh and elsewhere.

First, Grameen Bank, unlike many other poverty alleviation organizations, does not seek to provide an integrated package of poverty alleviation services to poor people. It is a bank and its main purpose is providing simple banking services. It takes small scale credit and savings directly to the poorest people. The service is offered; poor people decide themselves whether to take it. Organizing into groups and centers is a precondition for access to the service. Out of the groups and their strength may come a variety of secondary impacts, including the clients' growing confidence in their abilities and the opportunities to exercise entitlement to training and extension.

Other grassroots NGOs often have more complicated intervention models. They begin with interventions aimed at raising social consciousness and creating a basis for groups of poor people to plan and implement the development projects they decide on. In the process the NGOs expect to provide inputs to training, infrastructure, small scale credit, health services, water supply and other activities.

Secondly, and related to the first, Grameen Bank has a dual vision. It sees itself as a poverty alleviation organization, but it is also concerned with its commercial viability as a bank. The dual goals of commercial viability and poverty alleviation do not always run on parallel tracks. How the dual vision is managed is an important part of management at Grameen Bank.

A third key feature of Grameen Bank is its structure. New and experimental activities are structurally separated from the management of the basic task of providing banking services to the poor. The critical core work is insulated. Moreover, this core work is delegated to Zonal, Area and Branch units, each of which operate banking services autonomously within the larger structure. The responsibility for Grameen's core work is diffused and decentralized.

Notes

1. Barbara Crossette, "Bangladesh Chief Visits Washington", New York **Times**, 19 March 1992, 8.
2. A clear description of Grameen Bank as a model and as an organization appears in Andres Fuglesang and Dale Chandler, **Participation as Process** (Dhaka: Grameen Bank, 1988). Though this book, publication of which was supported by the Norwegian Ministry of Development Cooperation, is somewhat old, the functioning and philosophy of basic banking operations they describe remain essentially unchanged.
3. The term targeted rural credit has two implications. It refers immediately to credit aimed at or restricted to clients identified as poor. Not all observers believe that credit needs to be targeted in order to reach the very poor. In an unpublished paper Henry R. Jackelen and

Elisabeth Rhyne contend that "the most effective means of reaching the poor is to ensure that small loans (and savings services) will be granted efficiently". Henry R. Jackelen and Elisabeth Rhyne, "Towards a More Market Oriented Approach to Credit and Savings for the Poor". Unpublished photocopy, n.d. The other implication of targeted rural credit is, for some observers, the necessity of a target group, organized to enable participation of the poor. Aditee Nag Chowdhury, **Let the Grassroots Speak** (Dhaka: University Press Limited, 1989), 16-17.

4. Henry Jackelen, "Assessing the Ability of Grameen Bank to Diversify." Pre-formulation Mission Report: BGD/90/CO1 Grameen Irrigation Project, New York: United Nations Capital Development Fund, May 1988.

5. Translation based on Fuglesang and Chandler, **Ibid**, 127.

6. See the discussion in Aditee Chowdhury, **Let the Grassroots Speak**, 196.

7. Grameen Bank, **Phase III Preparation Report** 1989-1992 (Dhaka: Grameen Bank, 1988), 65-66.

8. This figure is adapted from that developed by Mintzberg in **The Structuring of Organizations** (Englewood Cliffs, N.J.: Prentice-Hall, 1979). It helps to give a perspective of the dynamics of management. In the case of Grameen Bank, Mintzberg's model illustrates the separation of the core work from the other parts of the organization.

9. Melanie S. Tammen, "Foreign Aid: Treating the Symptoms: Misunderstanding the Microenterprise", in **Reason** 22 (June 1990), 40-41.

10. Chowdhury, **op. cit.**, 167.

11. Notes taken by author from tape recorded interview of Mohammad Yunus by Barbara Doran, Dhaka: December 12, 1990.

12. He refers, for example, to the contention that the effects of rural credit should be measured in terms of additionality, or what would have happened had the credit not existed. "...but additionality is hard to measure at the farm level. Moreover the effect of credit can often be over-estimated." Mahabub Hossain, **Credit for Alleviation of Rural Poverty: The Grameen Bank in Bangladesh** (n.p.: International Food Policy and Research Institute in collaboration with the Bangladesh Institute of Development Studies, 1988), 55.

13. **Ibid**, 55-67.

14. Nazrul Islam, Amirul Islam Chowdhury and Khadem Ali, **Evaluation of the Grameen Bank's Rural Housing Programme** (Dhaka: Centre for Urban Studies, University of Dhaka, 1989), 22-23.

15. Atiur Rahman, "Human Responses to Natural Hazards: The Hope Lies in Social Networking". A paper submitted at the 23rd Bengal Studies Conference held in the University of Manitoba, Winnipeg, Canada, 9-11 June 1989 (Dhaka: Bangladesh Institute of Development Studies). Note Tables 8 and 11.

16. Hossain reports that "In 1983/84 there were an estimated 13.8 million rural households, of which 6.2 million belonged to the Grameen Bank target group. The number of agricultural labor households was estimated at 5.5 million, of which 3.78 million belonged to the Grameen Bank target group. Hossain, **op. cit.**, 47.

17. Constantina Safilios-Rothschild and Simeen Mahmud, **Women's Roles in Agriculture: Present Trends and Potential for Growth** (New York: UNDP and UNIFEM, 1989), 29.

18. The 21 percent remaining unemployed may have taken the loan in their own name for the use of a male family member. Hossain, **op. cit.**, 61-62.

19. **Ibid**, 63-64.

20. **Ibid**, 59.

21. Mohammad Yunus, Managing Director, Grameen Bank, Interview by author, Tape Recording, Dhaka, 12 December 1990.

22. Islam et al., **op. cit.**, 23.

23. Safilios-Rothschild, **op. cit.**, 25.

24. Mahbub Ahmed, "Status, Perception, Awareness and Marital Adjustment of Rural Women; The Role of Grameen Bank", mimeographed report obtained from Grameen Bank, 1985).

25. Hossain, **op. cit.**, 44-46.

26. Yunus, Interview by author, 12 December 1990.

27. Tammen, **op. cit.**, 41.

28. Henry Jackelen and Elisabeth Rhyne, **op. cit.**, 1990, 4-5.

29. **Ibid**, 12.

4

VISION AND VALUES: KNOWING WHERE TO GO AND HOW TO GET THERE

One of the generally amiable idiosyncrasies of man is his ability to expend a great deal of effort without much enquiring as to the end result.[1]

John Kenneth Galbraith

Vision and values can be fuzzy concepts, but neglecting them has costs. Development practitioners may become involved in specifying inputs and assuring implementation rates while forgetting where development efforts are supposed to be going, or how the form of implementation affects end results. Distance, time and their own structure often keep international and bilateral donors from understanding the role of vision and values in managing the implementation of a particular poverty alleviation program. The neglect of vision and values weakens successful implementation.

Vision and values are powerful tools for coordination and control of quality outputs. Vision can keep leaders at various levels of the organization focused on the end result. Values can shape the capacity of the organization to reach those end results.

The experience of Grameen offers specific lessons about the role of vision and values in an organization implementing successful poverty alleviation work. Grameen senior management have, and have long had, a clear understanding of where the organization is going, what it wants to achieve, and the values or norms of behavior and practice in the organization. It is clear about the basic work of the organization and the organizational norms or values that should govern action.

From a process perspective, Grameen leadership plays an explicit role in managing organizational vision and values. As the next several chapters will document, leadership has used many techniques to assure that vision and values are widely understood and shared by staff at all levels, and by the client members.

From a substantive perspective there is interaction between the organization's expressed vision of poverty alleviation, participation and empowerment and the values or norms of behavior in implementing Grameen Bank work. Just as the Grameen vision values the capacity of poor people to use credit productively, the organizational values of Grameen are based on a belief in the capacity of all staff to implement an innovative, labor intensive poverty alleviation effort.

Grameen Bank aims at and largely achieves consistency in its vision and values. There is broad consistency between the vision and values the organization holds with respect to clients and with respect to their own internal management practice. And there is consistency between the vision and values expressed by senior managers and those expressed by managers and staff at the operating level.

It is this consistency of vision and values, espoused and enacted, that provides the framework for participatory and empowering management practice and allows decentralization and autonomy at the operating level. In this way centralized management of vision and values creates the conditions that enable decentralization, creating a structure that is at once both loosely and tightly organized.

The substantive content of the strategically managed vision and values at Grameen offers lessons to the development community. One is the insistence of Grameen on targeting credit to the poor and of providing staff with a definition of poor that can be made operational in the context of daily work. Grameen Bank practices what Americans would call "affirmative action" for the rural poor. Secondly, the stated values and the everyday practices of the organization emphasize the centrality of the client and the importance of learning, listening and supporting behaviors by Bank staff.

Finally, there is a curious and intuitively unexpected characteristic of Grameen Bank vision. The Bank has a dual vision. It seeks to be both a bank and a poverty alleviation organization. It seeks commercial viability while serving poor people. There is a tension in this dual vision, but a tension that is creative. The dual vision effectively captures the basic belief of the Bank that poor people should not be objects of charity. Poor people have the capacity to be disciplined, to generate income and to be responsible for meeting the obligations of repayment and saving.

This chapter looks at the vision and values articulated by Bank staff from senior leadership to operating levels. Chapter 5 assesses how the values are practiced. Chapter 6 looks at how Grameen Bank inculcates and maintains organization vision and values.

Specifying Vision

Grameen Bank senior leaders have clear definitions of its basic services or products and a targeted clientele. Senior Managers are equally clear about their commitment to the dual aspects of poverty alleviation: income/asset increases and empowerment and participation. Central to the vision is the means by which Grameen Bank works to reach its dual poverty alleviation objectives. Grameen has identified credit as the leading edge or pivotal tool to produce the dual aspects of poverty alleviation. The credit mode of intervention represents a model of how to alleviate poverty, a model that was tested, refined and is now fully operational.

There is a tension built into the Grameen Bank vision. This tension comes from the here and now focus on delivering commercially viable and professionally managed credit and banking operations to rural poor to raise income, and the incremental or longer term objectives of empowerment and participation. The challenge for Grameen leadership is to manage this tension creatively so that a successful credit intervention also serves the longer term vision of political and social empowerment of the poor.

Targeting the Clients

The Grameen Bank vision is firmly fixed on its clients and the alleviation of their poverty. It is fueled by a leadership belief that "poverty can be removed from the earth" if there is "a vision that poverty is unacceptable."[2] Area Managers express similar optimism that they can change the socio-economic position of the 70 percent or more of the Bangladeshis they say are below the poverty line.[3] Area Managers are aware of research documenting the impact of Grameen Bank work on alleviating poverty and of the international attention given to Grameen. They see this as proof of the possibility that poverty can be eliminated.

Focusing on the poor has never been an issue for Grameen Bank. Founder Yunus always insisted on the importance of programs dedicated exclusively to the poor; "...if one mixes the poor and the non-poor within the format of a single program, the non-poor will always drive out the poor."[4] Targeting the poor is a characteristic of the leading NGOs in Bangladesh. Targets have been the principal mechanism for addressing gender issues in small scale credit management. Both Professor Yunus and his colleague, Mohammad Abed, who is head of the Bangladesh Rural Advancement Committee (BRAC), identify the use of targets (or quotas) as the reason for their extraordinary success in reaching women clients.[5] One argument is that targets provide a disciplined framework that reduces the possibility that richer or more powerful groups will hijack resources intended for the poor.

There are examples in other countries and cultures of successful, small scale credit that reaches the poor without having explicit targets. Bank Rakyat Indonesia (BRI) and Prodem in Bolivia are two examples of credit organizations that do not target the poor but succeed in reaching the poor. They may be less successful in reaching women borrowers. Only 25 percent of BRI borrowers are women (1990). The argument against targeting is that when small scale credit is offered efficiently to the poor, they will use it.[6]

Grameen has always had a concrete measurable definition of its target group of rural, landless poor. Originally the definition of poor was ownership of less than 0.4 of an acre of land. Today the operational definition of poor has been increased to holdings of less than 0.5 of an acre, or less than Tk. 20,000 (US\$570 at 1991 rate of US\$1.00 = Tk.35) in total assets. When asked, Area Managers echo the formal definition. In their daily work they are constantly operationalizing the definition. Along with Program Officers in the Area, Area Managers are responsible for recognizing the groups of five borrowers that form the basis of loans, and for approving loans. Both functions require effective Area Manager review of whether individual members meet eligibility requirements. The precision with which operating managers apply the asset criteria is open to question. From a management point of view, the criteria are well known, the process of assessing a prospective client against the criteria is a transparent one, and the staff members are exposed in their training to a variety of techniques for making the assessment.

Yunus himself sees that precise definition of the target group is important, not for theoretical reasons, but for operational efficiency. Staff need a standard against which to identify their clients. Without an objective standard staff might gradually slip into serving better-off clients without realizing what was happening.[7]

In specifying the poor as clients, Grameen is referring to the poor, one by one, not as a mass. "It is individuals who are trying to get out of poverty...so that you create more opportunities for people to do their things" rather than helping one or two people to hire others.[8] Yunus insists that he started Grameen Bank with a "worm's eye view", looking at real people and trying to understand poverty from the perspective of the individual. "If I can help one single person it is better than thinking about the whole nation".[9]

Grameen, as noted, has set gender targets for its operations in a culture where women have traditionally been shielded from public contacts. In the beginning the Grameen project identified women as a particular target because "...Bangladeshi bankers treated women as a second-level borrower or a dependent borrower. If a woman walked into a Bangladeshi bank to borrow, its manager would always ask whether her husband knows about it, too, and whether she would like to bring her husband along to talk about it."[10] Recognizing the difficulties of a predominantly male staff working with female clients, Yunus says that Grameen early on set itself a target of attracting 50 percent male and 50 percent female clients. That Grameen Bank staff have achieved a gender target at variance with practice in the surrounding society is apparent not only in the predominance of women among clients, but also in the use of the female pronoun when Area Managers speak about borrowers:

"...if a member is in trouble, everyone will help her."

"...the main purpose was to make her economically solvent."

Defining Basic Objectives

The key to understanding Grameen Bank's vision is in the creative tension between the narrow banking goals and the larger empowerment goals. While Grameen Bank has grown and changed since Professor Yunus' first experiments with small scale credit in the early 1970s, its basic vision remains the same. A document prepared in 1988 for a consortium of donors restated Grameen Bank's long-held objectives in a formal way:

- to extend banking facilities to poor men and women;
- to eliminate exploitation by moneylenders;
- to create small enterprise opportunities for the unemployed and underemployed;
- to bring disadvantaged people within the fold of some organizational format which they can understand and operate and can find some socio-political and economic strength through mutual support;
- to reverse the age-old vicious circle of "low income, low savings,

low investment, low income" into an expanding system of "low income, credit, investment, more income, more credit, more investment, more income".[11]

These objectives begin with the specific input of credit facilities for the poor and move through intermediate goals of elimination of exploitation by moneylenders, expansion of self-employment, and empowerment through group formation, to a new state that transforms the downward cycle of poverty into an expanding spiral of growth and development.

Grameen's origins explain the development of its founder's vision, and why he saw credit as the tool for economic change and empowerment. Mohammad Yunus finished his doctorate in economics at Vanderbilt University and returned to his country in the early 1970s. He began teaching at Chittagong University just as Bangladesh was emerging from the War of Liberation which gave it independence from Pakistan. He was full of hope for the capacity of the new nation to address the problems of poverty. By 1974 and the famine which occurred that year, Yunus had concluded that poverty was getting worse, not better. He was keenly aware of a gap between the economics he was teaching in the classroom and the economics experienced by poor people in the villages of Bangladesh. To study the economics of the poor, he went out to a village near the University of Chittagong campus using observation and informal interview techniques to determine why poor people are poor. He found that the poorest people were those without land. They survived on a variety of activities, and were often dependent on landowners or others in the village with capital. What the poor lacked was even a minimal amount of capital, perhaps only five or six dollars, to fund the raw materials for a small enterprise.

Yunus' training as an economist and his learning from village poor underpin his model of poverty alleviation. On one level the model is very simple. It says that credit is the simple intervention which will allow the poor to increase their income. By focusing on credit, this simple model seems to say that poverty alleviation is measured chiefly in terms of income changes. Seen this way, as it sometimes is, Grameen Bank appears to be in contrast to other poverty alleviation organizations whose model for poverty alleviation requires an integrated package of interventions that may include training, extension, physical inputs and consciousness raising as well as credit. These more complex models assume that multiple interventions are needed to achieve changes in the financial and power status of the poor.[12]

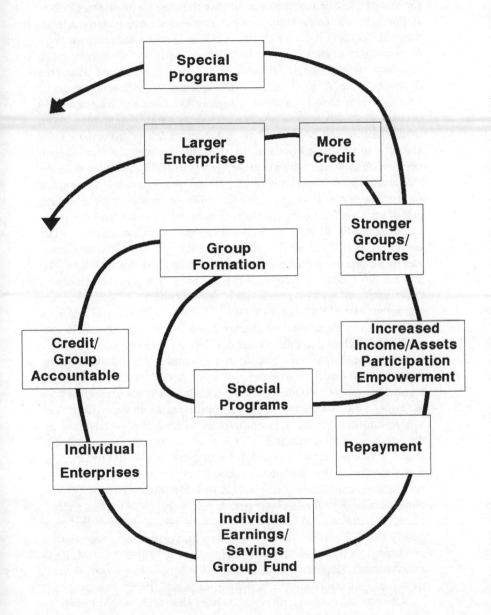

The distinction between simple and multiple intervention strategies for poverty alleviation is important for the development practitioner. If simple credit interventions are sufficient to achieve poverty alleviation, they are clearly economically efficient. From a management point of view, the single credit intervention is easier to implement. The Grameen Bank model, however, is more complicated than the description of it as a single intervention organization suggests. Grameen is a model based on assumptions about the inequalities in society which create and maintain poverty, and assumptions about human nature. It sees credit as a leading edge or pivotal tool for affecting those inequalities and for releasing the inherent capacities of people. A companion intervention, group formation, is central to the effectiveness of the credit tool. Group formation is a common mechanism for enabling participation. The existence of these groups and of group solidarity builds the access or ability to demand extension services, health services or a voice in local decision-making. The discipline of meeting weekly loan payments and of operating a small enterprise producing income creates new habits and expectations. The success of credit in raising income, even if only incrementally, contributes to self-awareness and empowerment. These in turn strengthen the effectiveness of credit. Instead of the stagnation of poverty, an upward spiral of change is set in motion. Data collected in this research suggest the model developed in Figure 4.

Professor Yunus says that in the beginning he did not see the importance of credit. Theoreticians, he says, did not identify credit as an obstacle facing individuals. In the economic literature, credit is seen as a lubricant of business. Yunus' observations in the village convinced him that "credit is an entitlement to resources"; "credit gives opportunity to individuals to establish their own human rights, to create their own income flow". Access to credit enables a small business, but it is something more than that. Access to credit is social power. The poor are generally denied that access or entitlement to credit. Credit empowers because it takes poor people seriously. This implies another set of assumptions. Offering credit to poor people assumes that poor people can and will pay back. It assumes that people have potential for producing, or as Yunus says are "a treasure of abilities".[13] Mohammad Mortuza, Deputy General Manager for Monitoring and Evaluation explained, the poor "are the best instruments of [their] own change."

Offering access to credit also assumes that poor people can discipline themselves to meet loan payments and to save. Mortuza believes that "through discipline the poor can change their lives, but that credit without discipline is charity."[14] Mozamul Huq suggested that "external discipline is important in a society which is totally undisciplined" noting the high rates of non-repayment of credit in the commercial and agricultural sectors.[15] Discipline is an essential element of the empowerment.

Banks re-enforce the lack of access or powerlessness of the poor. Banking theory is based on collateral. The poor and landless have no collateral. Therefore they are not creditworthy. Banks, especially in a poor society, are formal and formidable institutions, not welcoming to poor people. In these ways banks play a role in making one part of society rich while keeping the other poor.

Not only are banks anti-poor, Yunus asserts, they are anti-illiterate and anti-women. Only 23 percent of the Bangladesh population can read, but bank transactions are based on written documents. This effectively bars access to bank services for 77 percent of the population. Moreover, in Bangladesh, by tradition rather than by law, women need the consent of their husband, father or male guardian to borrow money. This limits the entitlement of the female half of the population, and particularly of poor female heads of household.[16] Yunus argues that societies must look at their basic concepts and institutions and ask why they serve one segment of society but not others. He says that Grameen has turned banking procedures upside down. Grameen staff take banking services to the clients in their village.

Credit as a means is empowering not only to the poor, but also to Grameen Bank as an institution. Several senior managers in interviews raised the disempowering aspects of development assistance. They argue that much development assistance goes into the pockets of donor contractors (international or local) or slips into the hands of the rich. This traditional pattern of bilateral and multilateral assistance fosters dependency. To the extent that donors demand conditionality, aid also perpetuates the reliance of the recipient on donor planning.

A credit approach can be institutionally empowering in two ways. First a commercially viable credit operation for the poor can, over time, reduce reliance on donors for funds. As credit and savings services become cost-covering and generate capital, outside capital can become less important. Second, a drive toward a self-sustaining or profitable enterprise may foster an attitude of independence and an ability to counter interference of outside donors in planning.

Having said this, it is not clear whether Grameen Bank credit and savings operations do, can, or even should, break even or make a profit. The question of the actuality or likelihood of Grameen branch profitability produces a variety of answers (see discussion in Chapter 3). To the extent that Grameen can achieve break-even banking operations it releases itself from dependence on donor subsidies. This is not unimportant. Here, however, the issue is not so much whether or when Grameen could achieve that break-even performance. The important issue is the extent to which leadership espouses self-sufficiency and independence as a guiding principle. The articulation of branch self-sufficiency as a goal is one example of how the vision of self-sufficiency is used to structure and discipline banking operation. It also illustrates the tension between the narrow banking operations and the larger empowerment goals of the bank.

Leadership at Grameen Bank speaks of moving Branch Banks toward a break-even or profitable point within six years (or seven to eight years, depending on the speaker) of founding. Several senior managers look forward to the time when Grameen banking operations will need no more funding from donors.

Internally the monitoring and evaluation staff have devised the concept of the "model branch" to identify which practices produce profitability and reduce costs. The model branch concept provides a basis for monitoring progress of individual branches toward profitability. The concept provides a goal and a structure for disciplined management of banking operations.[17]

At the same time, Grameen leadership recognizes the tension inherent between the drive for profitability of branches and the poverty alleviation goals of the organization. Grameen Bank data show that branch profitability is correlated with Branches having a high proportion of income from general and collective loans. General and collective loan income accounts for 68 percent of total income on average of the 125 profitable branches (1990). General loans are the most common form of loan, including all those loans made to individual members. Collective loans are less common and are made to a group of 20 to 30 to capitalize a larger activity.

Other Branches achieve rapid profitability through technical loans to the Studies, Innovation, Development and Experimentation (SIDE) program and to other enterprises with which Grameen is experimenting.[18] Because these loans are larger they produce a rapid increase in interest earning to the Branch granting them.

The Assistant General Manager for Planning, Masud Isa, noted that not all Branches are able to achieve a high level of general and collective loans, or have access to technical loans. Not all branches have the capacity to be profitable in the medium term. Nor should they be expected to be so in a poverty alleviation organization. Some Branches serve areas so lacking in economic potential that it is difficult for them to attract enough clients able to sustain large loans. The resulting small loan portfolio cannot generate enough income to cover Branch costs. The capacity for absorbing loans varies by situational factors. Zones in remote areas, where marketing facilities are limited, will expand loan disbursement more slowly. Rangpur and the northern areas, which are poor, will see slow change in disbursements. The challenge for senior management is to distribute the costs of slow developing areas.[19]

Grameen is experimenting with a model of the profitable Branch as a means to discipline and regulate banking operations. The donors have encouraged the development of the model branch concept as a tool "to help branch managers to achieve the organization's objectives of increasing the G&C (General and Collective) loans outstanding and membership" and as a means of moving toward profitability.[20] Branch profitability is an important goal. Grameen leadership does not want to see this commercial goal drive out long term poverty alleviation goals. This is most apparent in the way leadership manages the tension between the requirements of an efficient credit operation and the priorities of poverty alleviation goals. It is also apparent in the way leadership responds to donor monitoring of its credit and savings operations.

If achieving Branch Bank profitability were the dominating goal of Grameen Bank, then one might expect the leadership to set targets for increasing the loan portfolio, particularly general and collective loans, and thus the loan income of each Branch. It could link staff rewards (or sanctions) to the achievement of targets such as loan disbursements. In fact, senior management does not use targeted increases in Branch loans in this way. Chapter 8 describes how performance goals and other devices are used to control and coordinate the work of the Bank. Here the important point is that banking performance goals are an important part, but not the only part, of Grameen Bank vision.

Senior management balances branch performance and profitability against other factors. When asked about the model branch concept, Mozamul Huq, General Manager of the Grameen Bank, explained that simply increasing disbursements is not the priority. "If disbursement

67

is good and repayment is 100 percent, we are not impressed. The question is what has happened to the borrowers, what has been the impact on their lives." In terms of financial performance indicators, it is more useful to look at trends rather than at specific indicators. "In a branch which is more than three years old and has 250 groups, if the losses are still going up, then it is a matter for concern. Or compare the branch with a 100 percent repayment rate and an average loan of Tk.2,000 with another branch with a 100 percent repayment rate and an average loan of Tk.800. The second branch may actually be the better branch because it is truly reaching the poorest people. In this case the critical indicator is whether over time the Tk.800 Branch is able to raise the amount of the average loan".[21]

Vision at the Operating Level

Area Managers also identify this tension between the narrow objectives of disbursing and collecting loans and the broader social objectives. Area Managers in the focus group discussions in Rangpur said that "the collection of the loan is not the main purpose of Grameen Bank. The main purpose is to make the poor economically and socially solvent." Referring to a case where a woman's husband has run off with the Tk.3,000 she borrowed, they say that "the collection of the loan is not the main factor; how she will develop herself is more important".[22] An Area Manager from Tangail noted that "it is not just important to make profits for the Bank, but also to make loans to poor people, to keep them as borrowers".[23] For Area Managers, the commonly expressed goal of "helping the poor" is operationalized in both economic and socio-political terms, with activities being mutually supportive. An Area Manager in Bogra noted that in helping the poor to achieve their social and economic rights, Grameen Bank activities are ..."integrated. You cannot focus on a single activity; they are all important together". A colleague says "we must do all activities simultaneously to alleviate poverty. Which activity is most important it is difficult to say".[24] What are these activities essential to poverty alleviation? During the focus group discussions more than one Manager at two or more discussions identified the following: development of individual leadership; group formation and building group unity for joint action; encouraging individual and group discipline; raising consciousness about rights and possibilities, increased social status; encouraging savings; disbursing housing loans ("home mortgages"); initiating fisheries, pump and other economic projects; promoting community based education, family planning, health and hygiene education.

Managing Vision for the Future

Grameen senior leaders take an active role in shaping the future vision of the Bank. Field managers only rarely voice a strategic vision.

As the Bank gained experience with poverty alleviation and grew to a size where it operates in one third of the villages in Bangladesh, its vision of its role in poverty alleviation evolved. The Grameen Bank experiment began, as noted, with a focus on the poor as individuals and with moving the poor out of poverty, one by one. Today senior management expresses the conviction that Grameen Bank needs to begin to influence national policies. Khalid Shams, the Deputy Managing Director, made the argument for this evolving vision. Micro-level interventions will not achieve rapid change. He cited as important "...the policies of government which can bolster and support the efforts of the poor; the industrial policies, fiscal policies, credit policies, housing policies. Unless there is a distinct bias in favor of the poor, you're not going to achieve much change."

Shams identified a particular need for change in agricultural productivity. As Grameen has begun to work with funding and management of deep tube wells, it has seen the interconnection between its poverty alleviation efforts and government policy and programs. Unless agricultural productivity rises very quickly, there will be little impact on the incomes of the poor.[25]

Government practice at different levels may also be an obstacle to development efforts. The Ministry of Agriculture has vaccines and training capacity, but extension workers do not seek out poor women owners of cows or poultry. Grameen made an agreement with the National Fisheries Administration to take over management of fish ponds, but the local administration attempted to block its access to the ponds. Without solid support at the government level, development efforts can be frustrated. To open or protect opportunities for its clients, Grameen itself needs capacity to influence government. As Shams stressed, "Government is the most important actor in the development scenario...Unless there is a distinct bias in favor of the poor, you are not going to make much change. Even if there were ten Grameen Banks, you would not achieve a significant qualitative change in people's lives without change at the macro level".[26]

Mozamul Huq and others have suggested that Grameen Bank members are now ready for a larger role. Their experience of participating in center meetings, workshops and even in representation on the Board have helped them gain "the autonomy to protest", and Grameen Bank has provided the organizational structure to voice the protest. During the national election campaign in March 1991, Bank leadership encouraged Grameen Bank members to debate among themselves which of the candidates running in their District was most likely to support their interests. They urged members to vote and to vote in identifiable groups so that they could be identified as a significant political force at the local level. The vision emerging moves Grameen to a more political and policy role.

Articulating Values

The values that an organization espouses provide the framework for management behavior. As we shall see here and in the next Chapter, the values, or the articulated cultural assumptions of Grameen as an organization, differ from those of the larger Bangladeshi culture. Together, this section and the next chapter will explore the congruence between the expressed values and the values practiced by the organization. This section reports a remarkable similarity between values espoused by Grameen leadership and by Area Managers.

Grameen leadership has an expressed commitment to building and maintaining an organization culture that fosters learning and experimentation. It encourages openness, questioning, consultation, listening, and a team approach, reflecting an assumption that all individuals have an inherent capacity to contribute to deliberation and decision. Because it believes in the capacity of its staff, the leadership expects disciplined performance or professionalism. It expects responsibility and accountability.

These three categories of cultural assumptions are overlapping and interdependent. Experimentation and a learning process approach enable Grameen operations to find the best ways of solving problems and serving organization goals. Experimentation and learning are possible because of a belief in the usefulness of openness, questioning, a consultative approach, willingness to acknowledge mistakes, and a belief in the abilities of staff. Experimentation, openness, willingness to tolerate error in the learning process can operate because of a commitment to discipline and accountability for results. Area Managers' articulation of these three categories of organizational values in focus group discussions and individual interviews largely echoes the expression of senior management. Senior management appears to have successfully inculcated the "espoused values" of the organization (see Chapter 5).

A Learning Culture

Grameen's banking operations were born and developed through a learning process approach. The story of Grameen's founding and its experimental, learning process approach has entered the lore or mythology of Grameen Bank. But the basic banking operations, the product of past experimentation, are now an operational model fixed in its essentials open to adaptation chiefly at the margins. The present locus for experimentation in Grameen Bank are in the SIDE (Studies, Innovation, Development and Experimentation) program and the Technology Department. This research is focused on the banking operation.

Professor Yunus began the small scale credit operations as an experiment, persuading a bank to give small loans to poor borrowers on Yunus' responsibility. Through trial and error, the basic procedures of small scale lending and savings were developed and improved. Yunus had learned from earlier cooperatives in Bangladesh that borrowers' willingness to repay declines as the length of time before repayment is increased. At first he required daily repayment of Grameen loans. The administration of daily repayment was found to be too cumbersome, and so the practice changed to the current weekly repayment in center meetings. Over time Grameen managers decided that groups should be limited to five unrelated members.

By the mid-1980s, and as the Bank began more rapid expansion, the basic patterns of Branch Bank operations were developed and standardized. The same commitment to experimentation and learning by doing remains basic to any new activity Grameen undertakes. Its current efforts to develop the model branch concept which will allow it to predict loan and savings volumes are an example of the willingness to

test, correct and improve an undertaking until it performs to expectations.[27]

This trial and error approach is also reflected in the new technology
enterprises Grameen is initiating. For example, in 1985 Grameen Bank
took over the Joysagar Fish Farm from Government. It is a major
enterprise with a total of 807 ponds which had been established with
British assistance in the mid-1970s. Government management was
unable to sustain the fish farming activities. Equipment and facilities
fell into disrepair.

The Grameen Bank staff who manage the fish farm are all general-
ists. Two of them were given three months training in China at a
similar facility. In 1990 there were 80 Bank staff, 2,000 group
members from the target group and 538 ponds under development.
The Grameen Bank performed technical tasks including operations of
a hatchery and timing of feeding fish and of harvesting. Professor
Yunus regards the Fish Farm as a success story. In 1989 250 tons of
fish were harvested. A harvest of 600 tons was expected in 1990, and
the short term target is 1,000 tons. The largest harvest when the
government managed the Fish Farm was 50 tons.

The traditional development approach would have been to bring in
technical experts at the beginning of the Fish Farm project in order to
speed up productivity gains. Professor Yunus believes that this would
have been wrong. "Why? We feel that people have the ability. They
don't need training for everything...we could have brought experts in
when production was at the level of one half ton, but experts are
useless at that level. When we reach the production level of 1,000
tons, then we can talk to experts and ask how to take it beyond".[28]

The principle Grameen leadership espouses, and seems to practice,
is that learning or technical transfer is most effective when it is experi-
ence-based learning and when staff participate in the trial, error and
learning. Professor Yunus said that Fish Farm staff "had no experience of running anything. We learn as we go, changing rules,
adjusting." He believes that people can learn new processes. "We
were told the women couldn't operate rice mills, but now they are
doing it." He stresses that learning isn't instantaneous, "...it won't all
happen tomorrow." He adds, "We have never had experts" as he
explains why he has resisted taking funding from the World Bank.
"We love to make mistakes and correct them. We learn how the process works".[29] Senior management at Grameen Bank echoes Professor Yunus' commitment to a learning process approach, stressing the

importance of being able to learn in a world which is dynamic and changing.[30]

Area Managers do not talk about a learning process approach; instead they talk about the opportunities and even the necessity for attempting creative solutions to problems they themselves encounter and for which there are no set procedures. In the focus group discussions, Area Managers noted that while there is a lot of "scheduled" work, mostly in relation to banking functions, they frequently face unplanned situations. One gave the example of the group that took a loan to rent a paddy field for joint cultivation A flood made the field unusable and the group had no income to repay the loan. The Area Manager suggested fish farming as an alternative way to use the field while flooded. In another case, an epidemic appeared to be killing cows in a region; the Area Manager arranged for vaccine and training from the Ministry of Agriculture. Another Manager believed that several periodic reporting forms were redundant and so he felt free to propose an alternative, streamlined reporting form. Another identified child spacing and smaller families as critical issues in his area. He changed the normal reporting in weekly center meetings to monitor explicitly family changes. He encouraged family planning workers to attend center meetings.

Area Managers defined this opportunity for experimentation in terms of work they personally do (as opposed to work they manage). What they seemed to be saying is that there is considerable scope for innovation and creativity within the framework of the Grameen Bank credit model. They perceived that senior management has delegated the authority to experiment and that they are trusted to do so. Moreover, they clearly believed that experimentation, outside the core banking functions, is encouraged even if they did not articulate it as a learning process approach.

Valuing People Through Openness and Listening

Senior management frequently characterized Bank workers and clients as resources, "treasures" or opportunities. Area Managers' characterization of the people they work with, subordinates and clients, differed slightly from that of senior management. Area Managers were more likely to value good relations with subordinates and clients as a way of facilitating the work processes.

Most senior managers repeatedly referred to the innate capacities of lower level staff and of clients. As Yunus described it, "they have the ability" and they are in the position to solve the problem. "If you create an enabling environment, people are ingenious; when there is a problem, they come up with a solution".[31] Other senior managers told stories of how Bank Workers or Branch Managers encountered problems in unstructured situations and come up with solutions. They pointed to the methodology of staff training (see Chapter 6) which assumes that staff have the capacity to find the answers for themselves.

Both Senior Managers and Area Managers spoke of the importance of good human relations with staff and clients to the smooth operation of Grameen Bank work. Senior management characterization of staff relations focused on the importance of the work of the lowest level, while the Area Managers statements showed concern for efficiency and teamwork and for an ideology of brotherhood and equality. The Deputy Managing Director, for example, talked about the assumptions underlying training. The training does not teach new recruits a highly specified or ritualized work routine. Training seeks to build a frame of mind that enables (or empowers) the Bank staff to become professionals, solving problems. The emphasis of training is not on learning things, but on learning the tools of defining problems, drawing inferences, and developing solutions.[32] The training perceives Bank staff as actors rather than ciphers.

For Area Managers, valuing staff is valuing good relations with them. If there is not a good relationship between a boss and subordinate, one Area Manager noted, the latter will not freely carry out the boss's order. Another saw good relationships as basic to teamwork, and that teamwork is more efficient than individuals working alone. Another suggested that without behaving like a gentleman, one cannot be a good manager.

Many Area Managers used the same language to describe the ideal relationship among staff. "We are all brothers here and we'd like to create such an environment which makes employees feel like brothers." Others referred to bank staff as "family". One noted that Managers and Bank Assistants share the same conditions of work. He suggested that when in the early morning a Bank Assistant walks to a center meeting with a Branch or Area Manager, that worker thinks, "This man is highly dignified, a master's degree holder, and he is going with me. In the rainy season he takes off his shoes and walks in the mud.

There is no difference between officer and worker."

Many Area Managers maintained that they took specific actions to build good human relationships with staff. Many said they made a point of shaking hands with Branch staff whenever they made a visit; of trying to engage as many staff as possible in personal as well as professional discussion.

Senior Management values people as a "treasure of ability". To access those abilities, they want to build in Grameen a culture of openness and questioning, which, they say, contrasts with that of the surrounding culture. "In Grameen Bank there is freedom to write, doubt, criticize." While the senior management have mostly had long ties and deep respect for the Managing Director, "...they do not unquestioningly accept commands or accede to all his requests." These people question, they argue, debate and criticize in discussions with the Managing Director. This would never happen in government in Bangladesh, one senior manager said, because the culture of the government mandates deference and acquiescence to those higher in the hierarchy. A government officer would show outward respect and not criticize. Decision-making in Grameen, by contrast, he says, is collegial and consultative. Major policy decisions are discussed and drafted in committee. Proposals are circulated for inputs. The Managing Director may present a problem to senior staff and ask for their recommendations in writing. Meetings and workshops are key mechanisms for consultative decision-making at the Zonal, Area and Branch levels. Within the Branches and even centers, decision-making on routine and non-routine matters is consultative, involving subordinate staff and clients.

For consultation to have meaning, it must be accompanied by the manager's capacity to listen. Failures of consultation, some senior managers said, are frequently a result of inability to communicate, of the failure of managers to "get their [subordinates'] ideas, to get their reactions" and to find the reasons behind the problem. This ability to communicate and listen was seen as a kind of leadership which transforms the poor.[33] Concerned about staff capacity to listen, senior management has introduced listening skills into the in-service training for Branch Managers.[34]

Some Area Managers also pointed to the importance of listening, and of creating the conditions where subordinates can speak freely. When good human relations exist, one Area Manager said in a focus group discussion, subordinates will raise problems and try to solve them instead of trying to hide them.

The learning process, openness, consultative and teamwork values espoused and practiced by the leadership promote participation and empowerment. They also imply responsibility and accountability. Leaders have a responsibility to communicate and listen. If a core assumption of the organization is that all individuals are a "treasure of ability" or have inherent capacities, then the responsibility of leaders is to unleash those capacities. When a Branch is doing well, you praise the Branch Manager. When the Branch is doing poorly, you blame the Area Manager. When the Area is doing well, you praise the Area Manager. When it does poorly, blame the Zonal Manager.[35] Responsibility is part of the disciplined professionalism of Grameen.[36]

Chapter 8 looks at the techniques management uses to keep Grameen Bank staff accountable for goals. The immediate issue here is whether managers espouse the notion of accountability or responsibility for results. Senior managers see responsibility or accountability as measured by changes in the condition of poor people. Yunus lists a number of indicators against which Grameen Bank work can be held accountable: such as repayment rates, attendance rates at centers. While Grameen Bank is proud of its high repayment rate, he said, that is not what is important. The key measure of accountability is whether the people are moving forward. The Sixteen Decisions are the best measure of real change in people's lives.[37]

Mozamul Hug linked Grameen's management information system, and the data it provides for a large number of performance indicators, to accountability. His explanation suggests the way in which accountability is decentralized and diffused. Accountability becomes the responsibility of the individual field manager and field worker. He points out that the differences among Areas and among Branches make comparisons difficult. Area Managers, however, have the figures that they can use to assess performance against the goals important for a particular Branch or Area. The responsibility rests with the Area Managers to use the data to manage performance. Accountability is pushed onto the Area Managers, and they are given the information to monitor their own performance.[38]

In the focus group sessions Area Managers were asked what indicators they used to judge operation of a Branch, or what are the signs of a good Branch. Area Managers readily described a variety of indicators they use on an individual visit: adherence to plans or schedules; loan repayment performance; disbursement rates; status of record-keeping; staff relationships. There was a recurring theme as Area Managers described indicators of performance. This was the concept of discipline. This meant discipline of the centers in terms of meeting attendance, participation in meetings, and regularity of savings and repayment. For staff it meant discipline in assuring proper functioning of centers, proper maintenance of records, support of Grameen's social programs, and particularly the Sixteen Decisions.

Conclusion

Senior management at Grameen have clearly articulated organizational vision and values. The target group, or customers, are specified in ways that can be acted on by staff at the operating level. The basic work of the organization, small scale credit taken to the poor, is clearly defined. Senior management demonstrates a clear understanding of the tension between Grameen's status as a bank and its poverty alleviation mission. They are able to identify the tension in the Bank's dual vision of a viable credit operation and a poverty alleviation organization. They propose that this tension is creative and re-enforcing of the mission to support disciplined and self-sufficient client/members.

The organizational values espoused by senior management - experimentation, learning from mistakes, and valuing the capacities of staff to be responsible and accountable for quality work - are consistent with the vision of the organization for its clients.

One role of senior leadership is to manage the vision and values. This means assuring that vision and values are widely shared throughout the organization. In this respect they appear to be largely successful. There is remarkable consistency between the vision and values articulated by senior management, and those expressed by field managers.

Finally, senior leadership fills the special function of managing the evolution of organizational vision and values to respond to changes in the operating environment and to the development of Grameen.

Notes

1. In United Nations Development Programme, **Guidelines for Project Formulation** (New York: UNDP, 1976), section 634000.

2. Mohammad Yunus, Managing Director, Grameen Bank, Speech, Notes by author, Washington, D.C., 4 October 1990.

3. Focus group discussions, Grameen Bank Zonal Meetings, Bogra, Rangpur, Dinajpur and Dhaka, conducted by author and research assistant, 3, 6, 8 April, 2 May 1991.

4. Muhammad Yunus, "On Reaching the Poor", speech presented at the Project Implementation Workshop, International Fund for Agricultural Development, Delhi, April 1984.

5. Interview by author, New York, 1 August 1991 and 16 July 1991, respectively.

6. Henry R. Jackelen and Elisabeth Rhyne, "Toward a More Market-Oriented Approach to Credit and Savings". Unpublished photocopy, n.d.

7. Yunus, "On Reaching the Poor", 8.

8. Mohammad Yunus, "Credit for Self-Employment of the Poor", Transcript of telephone press conference, Washington, D.C., 22 July 1987.

9. Mohammad Yunus, Managing Director, Grameen Bank, Interview by Barbara Doran, Notes by author from tape recording, Dhaka, 9 December 1990.

10. Yunus, "Credit for Self-Employment".

11. Grameen Bank, Preparation Report, 21. See also Yunus, "On Reaching the Poor".

12. See also Jackelen and Rhyne, **op. cit.,** who argue that credit and savings services should not be integrated into larger and more ambitious schemes; and Andres Fuglesang and Dale Chandler, in **Participation as Process--What We Can Learn From Grameen Bank Bangladesh** (Dhaka: Grameen Bank, 1988), who suggest a reassessment of the conscientization approach to poverty alleviation, 24-25.

13. Mohammad Yunus, Managing Director, Grameen Bank, Interview by author, Dhaka, 12 December 1990.

14. Mohammad Mortuza, Deputy General Manager, Grameen Bank, Interview by author, Dhaka, 17 March 1991. Discipline is one of the central values of Grameen culture.

15. Mozamul Huq, General Manager, Grameen Bank, Interview by author, Dhaka, 19 April 1991.

16. Yunus, Speech, Washington, 4 October 1990; Interview by author, 12 December 1990.

17. Yunus, Interview by author, 4 October 1990; Huq, Interview by

author, 19 April 1991; Mortuza, Interview by author, 17 March 1991; Dipal Chandra Barua, Deputy General Manager, Administration, Grameen Bank, Interview by author, Dhaka, 23 March 1991; and Masud Isa, Assistant General Manager, Planning, Grameen Bank, Interview by author, Dhaka, 25 April 1991.
18. Grameen Bank, Phase III Annual Review Mission, Final Report, November 1990, 7ff.
19. Isa, Interview by author, 25 April 1991; Mortuza, Interview by author, 17 March 1991.
20. Grameen Bank, Phase III Annual Review Mission, Final Report, November 1990.
21. Huq, Interview by author, 19 April 1991.
22. Focus group discussion, Rangpur Zonal Meeting, 6 April 1991.
23. Aminul Islam, Informal interview by author, Bhuyapur, 29 April 1991.
24. Focus group discussion, Bogra Zonal Meeting, 3 April 1991.
25. Khalid Shams, Deputy Managing Director, Grameen Bank, Interview by author, Dhaka, 20 March 1991. This corresponds with the assessment of Bangladesh economist, Mahabub Hossain, that an increase in the size of local markets and purchasing power is needed to enable expansion of small non-farm enterprises financed by Grameen loans. To do this an increase in agricultural productivity and income is needed. Mahabub Hossain, **Credit for Alleviation of Rural Poverty: The Grameen Bank In Bangladesh** (n.p.: International Food Policy and Research Institute in collaboration with the Bangladesh Institute of Development Studies, 1988), 37.
26. Shams, Interview by author, 20 March 1991.
27. Mortuza, Interview by author, 17 March 1991; Annual Review Mission, Working Paper No. 1 "Review of Financial Performance and Projections", Grameen Bank, November 1990.
28. Yunus, Interview by Barbara Doran, 4 December 1990; and visit by author to Joysagar Fish Farm, 6 and 13 December 1990.
29. Yunus, Interview by author, 12 December 1990.
30. Barua, Interview by author, 23 March 1991.
31. Yunus, Speech, Washington D.C., 4 October 1990.
32. Shams, Interview by author, 20 March 1991.
33. Shams, Huq, Mortuza and Barua, Interviews by author, 20 March, 19 April, 17 March and 23 March 1991.
34. Huq, Interview by author, 19 April 1991.
35. Huq, Interview by author, 19 April 1991.

36. Mohammad Yunus, Managing Director, Grameen Bank, Interview by author, Dhaka, 24 March 1991.
37. Yunus, Speech, Notes by author, 4 October 1990.
38. Huq, Interview by author, 19 April 1991.

5

MANAGING TO EMPOWER: PRACTICING WHAT THEY PREACH

"Empowering" really boils down to "taking seriously"[1]

Managing the implementation of a poverty alleviation effort requires consistency between the values espoused by the organization and the values actually practiced. The experience of Grameen Bank illustrates what this consistency means, and how it empowers staff at the level of operations.

To turn stated values into practice, Grameen Bank leadership is managing a culture change. Leadership manages a process that encourages field managers to adopt behaviors that may diverge from the norm in the larger society, but which converge with stated organization values. This chapter examines whether and in what ways behavior of Grameen field managers converges with articulated corporate values.

Success in creating a distinct organization culture - in encouraging behavior that converges with organization values - is the basis for structuring and coordinating the core work of the organization. The more successful management is at managing the culture or values that underpin the behavior of field staff, the less senior management needs to get involved in the substance of the tasks. This chapter looks at the key ways field manager practices reflect, or do not reflect, the espoused values of the organization. To what degree has Grameen Bank created a new culture?

Management Values and National Culture

Susan Davis, a recent Ford Foundation Program Officer in Dhaka, suggested that Grameen leadership is consciously managing its own culture. It is trying to establish a pattern of open communication that goes against the whole tradition of organizing society in Bangladesh. It is trying to create new norms of management within the old system.[2]

Managing to Empower

Observers of development management elsewhere have noted the consequences of failure to take into account the cultural assumptions of the outside society that permeate behavior inside the organization. The introduction of Western management innovations may be impeded by deeply rooted cultural assumptions about authority and communication.[3] Organization and societal culture can be in conflict, and the latter can overwhelm the former.

In Bangladesh, the societal culture or underlying assumptions about behavior do diverge in important ways from the values articulated by Grameen Bank. It is neither possible nor intended to give here a complete analysis of Bangladeshi culture. Some generalizations, while they ignore variations by location, class or economic activity, do highlight the specific divergence between Grameen Bank articulated values and the surrounding cultural assumptions that are relevant to this research. Fatalism, hierarchy, and the subservient role of women characterize Bangladeshi culture. Bangladeshi culture, like any other, is constantly changing. Education and growing urban residence tend to reduce the power of traditional culture. Nonetheless traditional culture represents the values to which most Bangladeshis have been socialized.

For the vast majority of Bangladeshis, Abecassis suggested, fatalism is "a mechanism for coping with deprivation, a response to the continuing realities of poverty and powerlessness".* One is poor because that is what Allah willed. "It is then a very short step to believing that one cannot do anything to change the situation, so that the belief becomes also that he will always be poor." The experience of rural development efforts in Bangladesh reinforces this notion of fatalism, at least so far as the poor are concerned. The Comilla project, well known among the rural development projects in Bangladesh, is only one example of poverty alleviation efforts where the benefits were captured by the rural rich.

Hierarchical relationships determine the organization of society in Bangladesh and the status of individuals within that society. Status is an important goal, Abecassis pointed out, for "the more status one has, the more respect one is given and the fewer demeaning incidents occur in one's social life; and the more opportunities to gain power and resources can be engineered." Jati, caste, or the group into which one is born, remains a determinant of status even though the majority of

---

*Much of the discussion here and all of the quotations are taken from the work of David Abecassis. See note 4.

Bangladeshis have long been Moslem. Landowning, education, wealth and power also contribute to place in the hierarchy. What is important here is that position in the hierarchy mandates social behaviors specifically suited to one's rank, and the rank of others involved in a transaction. The hierarchy creates patron - client relationships. Subordinates treat superiors with deference and respect; superiors may dominate subordinates. "There is a sense in which normally the client very much 'looks up' to his patron, recognizing him as a superior being and himself as an inferior being."

Related to questions of hierarchy are beliefs about the status of women. Abecassis argues that "the reality of a poor woman's life is very commonly that she is regarded in every way as an inferior form of human life." The perception of women as inferior stems from a deep-seated belief that they are polluted. Along with low status, women are subject to purdah or the practice of seclusion, severely restricting the capacity of women to participate outside the household.[4]

Grameen Bank managers are products of their own society. Of 67 Grameen field officers surveyed, 82 percent indicated that they had grown up in a rural area (as opposed to a small town or city) and 52 percent indicated that their fathers were farmers. Few Grameen staff come from the large cities. It is possible to assume that Grameen managers therefore were largely socialized in traditional culture in their pre-university years and that entrance into the Grameen culture, with its modernizing aspects, represents a change. The interesting observation about Grameen is their reliance on people from rural areas as agents of change and development. It is the induction of staff of rural origin into organization culture that allows these staff members to play the modernizing role.

Enacting a Culture of Learning and Experimentation

Much of what has been written about poverty alleviation work stresses the importance of a learning process approach and of experimentation and adaptability. The previous chapter suggested that an experimental or learning process approach characterized the founding of Grameen Bank and the development of its basic operating technology. It pointed to continuing senior management commitment to using an experimental or learning process approach in new ventures such as fish farming or management of Deep Tube Well schemes.

Managing to Empower

The commitment to experimenting and learning is rooted in the mythology of Grameen Bank. Managers and Bank Workers in the field spontaneously tell stories that give immediacy to leadership's commitment to experimenting and learning. One Area Manager recalled his first assignment to go out and open a new Grameen Bank Branch. He was nervous and asked for advice on how he should go about it. Professor Yunus sent him off saying that he would figure everything out when he got there. And, the Manager continued, "I did". Another story also refers to the founder. When Grameen was just beginning, Professor Yunus told his staff that he did not know how the project would develop but that they should go out and create Grameen. Most managers had similar stories about Professor Yunus or other senior managers who had been with Grameen since its founding days.

The ideals and myths of experimenting and learning are reflected in the everyday core work of Area Managers. They appear, however, not as carefully designed activities to test new types of interventions or alternatives to the core work, but as an attitude or willingness to try new approaches, to suggest or initiate incremental changes to the existing core work. Grameen Bank's core work, its credit operations, is itself no longer experimental. The basic technology or standard operating procedures for credit functions were established in the early 1980s. Experimentation on new types of Grameen activities takes place in separate units of Grameen Bank, most particularly in SIDE (Studies, Implementation, Development, Experimentation); the operating core is for the most part insulated from the experimentation. The fish pond development, the Deep Tube Wells, milling equipment and other enterprises are operated as separate projects. When aspects of these projects are introduced into the work of Area Managers, as in the case of Deep Tube Wells in Tangail Zone, it is done as a policy decision by senior management and as an experiment of senior management to determine whether Area Managers in a well-established zone can assume responsibility for a new enterprise.

Where, then, is the place for experimentation and learning by field level managers? Observations of Area Managers at work indicate that experimentation and learning is evidenced by a willingness to draw on a range of actions to respond to situations, incidents, problems or opportunities. The actions, for the most part, are not new. Most of the actions have been tried by Area Managers elsewhere. Area Managers have learned about successful responses to problems or opportunities and added them to their own repertory of actions.

In interviews and focus groups discussions, Area Managers identified these creative actions that originated with one of their colleagues who experimented, who was willing to take a risk on his or her own or who got permission to experiment. Many Area Managers expressed their own interest in pioneering a new approach, and identified what they are doing that they consider experimental or innovative in carrying out the core bank work. The prevailing attitude expressed was that Grameen encourages experimentation with different approaches so that the individual manager can find the best way to manage the core work. Experimentation, in other words, is flexibility and adaptation rather than formal testing of completely new interventions. Examples from Area Manager actions observed illustrate this.

All Area Managers observed adapted common solutions to common problems. In all Areas, a principal use of loans is for purchase of a cow; less frequently for other animals. Disease puts the animal at risk. In several centers where Area Manager visits were observed, there were reports of cows dying. In all cases the Area Managers were taking actions to assure borrower access to vaccinations, and in most cases arranging for training of a vaccinator from among the center members, and for supply of vaccines.

Other actions were similar. Confronted by reports of house fires during the dry season, one Area Manager used it as an opportunity to instruct all Branches to advise clients on fire prevention techniques. Concerned with meeting Grameen Bank objectives of family spacing and sanitary latrines, Area Managers institute devices like registers of births to track family growth; they arrange for family planning field workers to attend weekly center meetings; or they initiate a new form of loan for a sanitary latrine. None of these actions are standard Grameen procedure. They appear to become common practice, spread by word of mouth.

The practice of making loans to children illustrates the interest of managers in trying new ideas. The idea of making loans to poor children to enable them to carry on a small business, such as keeping small animals, is said to have originated with an Area Manager with many underemployed, poor children in his area. He wanted both to give children access to small credit that would allow them to generate income, but also to introduce them to the discipline of repayment and saving. He requested and received permission to try lending to children. With news of his success, interest in children's loans as a new form of loan disbursement spread and managers asked for guidance on procedures.

Managers also are interested in experimenting with or adapting the standard operating procedures. One Area Manager volunteered the information that he had written to the Managing Director recommending changes in how loans are disbursed to individuals and groups. Another Area Manager, in introducing a Bank Assistant, noted that the latter had proposed a consolidation of monthly reports and designed and sent a new reporting form to the Managing Director. The Head Office, he said, had duplicated and was now testing the form. Managers confirmed that writing to the Managing Director is a widely accepted mechanism for proposing new ideas. Several pointed out that the Managing Director has a "one man cell" to process mail.

Managers tell stories about the Managing Director's willingness to look at new ideas. One quotes the Managing Director as saying:

> If a proposal comes from the field to me and a high official drops it into the waste basket saying that it is a proposal by a mad man, and if in the course of time it is proved that the proposal is not mad but good, then that person who dropped it into the waste basket will be treated as mad.[5]

Several Area Managers referred to **Uddog**, the Grameen Bank house organ, as another way in which field staff at all levels could propose and circulate new ideas. One Area Manager pointed out an article he had written in **Uddog** containing his proposals.

The surrounding culture and recent development history in Bangladesh may tend to reinforce a sense of fatalism and deference to one's superiors that would seem to discourage field level managers and staff from raising and initiating new approaches. Inside Grameen, mechanisms such as **Uddog** and the tradition of writing to the Managing Director contribute to the building of a culture that encourages innovation and experimentation. Even if the experimentation is limited to innovations within the framework of standard operations, positive attitudes to change and a belief that subordinates can express ideas to superiors, that subordinates can influence changes, exist inside Grameen culture. The belief is reflected in the actions suggested by the examples above.

Willingness to learn has been associated with openness to acknowledging problems and adapting actions to what was learned. Two types of incidents illustrate the range of Area Managers' willingness to confront problems and errors and to learn from them. The first type includes incidents where Area Managers appear open to identifying mistakes, not necessarily in their own Area or field of responsibility, from which they have learned. In the case of Deep Tube Wells in Tangail Zone, the Area Managers observed explained their present actions - frequent visits to deep tube well staff - as a response to what they had learned from problems in the past. Under an agreement with the Bangladesh Agricultural Development Corporation, Grameen had taken over management and rehabilitation of 216 deep tube wells in Tangail. The scheme included the involvement of Grameen Bank members in the operation of the DTW irrigation schemes with Grameen playing a management role.

The 1990 operations were marked by corruption both by Grameen staff and by landholders who successfully avoided paying the agreed upon share of the crop. The existence of corruption was troubling in itself. It represented a break with Grameen's record of staff integrity. Staff corruption also contributed to failure of DTWs to meet their initial profitability objectives. Grameen senior management were first to identify and learn from the experience of corruption. They made changes in the number and potential of wells managed, in responsibility for management, and in the numbers of workers assigned. In Tangail Zone, managers were given greater responsibility for supervising the deep tube wells. Both Area Managers observed in Tangail volunteered information about past problems with corruption among Grameen staff. They explained that they make frequent visits to deep tube well staff in order to maintain the morale of deep tube well workers living at the well site under difficult conditions. At the visits they sometimes prepared the workers for supervising the collection of shares from the landholders at harvest time in order to reduce potential for cheating. The two managers observed spent 4-5 percent of their total work time at the deep tube wells during observation.

There were other examples where Area Managers showed keen awareness of problems in other areas. Several Area Managers noted management practices that contributed to poor loan repayment rates. One noted problems in a neighboring Zone where Branch Managers were encouraged to increase the rate of disbursement of loans, leading some branches to make loans larger than the Bank borrowers could carry. Another manager identified a Branch that had experienced repayment problems because of haste to disburse increasingly larger loans. The problem was reduced when the speed and size of disbursement was reduced.

The ability to learn is also demonstrated by the openness with which Grameen staff talked about problems or errors. This willingness was demonstrated most vividly in the range of ways managers were prepared to talk to an outsider and with subordinates about efforts to form a trade union among Bank Workers. Coincident with the beginning of this study, leaders of an effort to organize a trade union in Grameen Bank made public their demands that Grameen adhere to government regulations on working hours and overtime. News of the emerging trade union and uncertainty about its purposes and sources of funding represented a crisis for Grameen. There was evidence that the union movement within Grameen was financed by outside political interests. Senior management expressed concern that a trade union in Grameen, like other trade unions in Bangladesh, would serve political functions rather than the interests of workers. Nonetheless, formation of the union raised real problems for management, especially in light of reports that 60 percent or more of Grameen staff had indicated their support for the trade union. Finally, union demands for fixed working hours that mirrored the narrow limits of government regulations threatened the flexibility of staff to carry on field-based banking suited to the timing of poor farm laborers, or to return to centers in the late afternoons to work with members on social projects.

Grameen leadership had reacted openly to the unionization effort. Senior management met with the union leadership. The Zonal Managers had several meetings with the Managing Director and Head Office senior managers on strategy. They prepared a counter proposal for a Grameen workers association (*samiti*) and asked Zonal Managers to communicate with all their managers, urging them to discuss the trade union with Bank staff and to try to understand the concerns of those staff supporting the union. The Managing Director and his senior staff were open in discussing the trade union with the author and encouraged discussion of it with the Zonal Managers.

Management Behaviors That Empower Staff

If field staff can be the source of creativity and flexibility that allow a poverty alleviation organization to adapt, take advantage of opportunities, and achieve objectives, how does management empower the field staff to exercise that creativity and initiative?

Grameen management relies on a range of techniques to create an environment that encourages and empowers lower level staff to use their creativity and initiative to achieve organizational goals. Among these are basic management or leadership practices and skills. They include listening to and recognizing staff performance as well as structuring opportunities for staff to give feedback. In the Bangladesh context, Grameen practice gives special attention to actions that break down hierarchical relationships and promote equal interchange between staff at different levels. Those managers observed who were most successful at listening, recognizing and non-hierarchical behaviors were those who structured their routine work to include listening and time for feedback and recognizing performance. They took special actions to assure the participation of women staff, or of quiet staff. They also professed to be modelling these management practices on senior managers they regarded as being good leaders. Finally, field manager time is structured so that a large portion of their time is spend with subordinates and/or clients.

Listening

All six of the managers observed during the research for this book engaged in listening to subordinates and clients. What distinguished the nature of the listening was the ability and willingness of some managers to ask questions and to engage others in a dialogue, as well as an ability to refrain from lecturing. The two best listeners observed asked questions that invited longer answers and created an atmosphere that encouraged dialogue. Where this spirit existed, subordinates were ready to raise problems for discussion.

The observations coincided with the April Annual Confidential Reviews and promotions for those eligible. Promotions and pay were on the minds of many staff members. In all cases, subordinates did raise these issues. In the case of three Area Managers, the Bank Assistants and Branch Managers raised their questions in groups or individually in ways that suggested they would get support, help or information from the manager. With a fourth manager, some of the questions were about the basic procedures of promotion, suggesting that the subject had not been discussed before. In the remaining two cases Bank Assistants raised their concerns somewhat defensively and in the context of discussion on the trade union. In one case, Branch Managers frequently sought out the manager in his office or home to discuss their situation privately.

Where managers did not create the environment for listening to subordinates, they may have lost opportunities for learning or influencing. A Bank Assistant who is also a union organizer came to see his Area Manager one night. The manager lectured the Bank Assistant on the evils of the union rather than exploring the reasons for the assistant's involvement. Also working in the same manager's office was another union activist. The activist talked to others about union activities and concerns, but he said that the manager who shared the same working premises never discussed with him his union involvement. In the Areas of the two managers who demonstrated good listening skills and easy communication with staff, there was little union activity.

Those managers who listened effectively, talked least. When they spoke it was to convey information on a new procedure or to motivate subordinates or clients to new actions. Even when speaking, these managers would attempt to engage their listeners. For example, in explaining a method for ensuring that Grameen Bank got its fair share of the crop from deep tube well irrigated fields, one manager drew a diagram for Bank Assistants and invited their comments. Others interposed explanations of procedures with small talk or questions of personal relevance.

On the other end of the spectrum, a manager was observed talking at great length and listening little. Yet even this manager, who sometimes seemed to use his position for a soapbox, had great personal commitment to poverty alleviation and demonstrated his capacity to use questioning instead of lecturing. At one center eligible to receive its first housing loan, he helped members make their own decision as to which one of their members should get the first housing loan. Asking questions about the quality of housing of each member, he led them to the conclusion that the member with the thatched roof (the poorest housing) should be considered for a housing loan before those with tin roofs.

Feedback

Grameen has created a number of traditions that structure opportunities and even incentives for managers to listen, and that make it easier for subordinates to voice concerns or questions. A common practice is for subordinates to submit written, anonymous questions before meetings or workshops with superiors. The anonymity of the questions allows staff to raise difficult and contentious issues with superiors. The manager will then answer the questions before the group. The Managing Director uses this technique at weekly graduation ceremonies at the training institute and on his visits to the field. Zonal and other managers use it as a legitimized tool of communication. As described earlier, there is a well-established, and well-used, tradition in Grameen Bank of lower level staff writing to the Managing Director or other senior managers about ideas, problems or complaints.

Giving Recognition

Those managers with listening skills were in most cases also most likely to praise and encourage subordinates and clients, and less likely to blame or publicly humiliate them. Four managers tended to give praise for good performance in a public fashion. Sometimes it was complimenting a Bank Assistant in front of his Branch Manager for the good discipline of the center; other times it was praising a center or a group chairman for their knowledge of the Sixteen Decisions, or for the way they led the opening and closing of weekly meetings. The presence of an outside researcher was used occasionally to praise publicly the work of a Branch Manager; more often the outsider's visit was cited as proof of an international importance of Grameen Bank that reflected well on staff and members. The two managers with operational responsibilities for Deep Tube Wells gave priority to drawing attention to the work of DTW Bank Assistants and the difficulty of their working conditions and urging other staff to support them. Support to subordinates and clients was evidenced by willingness to help solve problems. Three of the Branches visited had just been audited and received reports detailing problems identified and corrections to be made. In two of the cases, the Area Manager worked with the Branch Manager to respond to the audit, exhibiting a "we're in this together" attitude.

When confronted with problem performance by a subordinate or a center, most managers tried to guide rather than to blame. An example in one Branch Bank where repayments had been irregular illustrates this guidance. Members would make token payments throughout the year, repaying the balance in a large lump sum at the end of the loan. There was evidence that the borrowers' enterprises were not generating enough income to make regular payments and that borrowers were taking a short term loan (perhaps from a moneylender) to pay off debt in order to be eligible for a new, and perhaps larger, Grameen Bank loan. The manager in this Branch was recommending new, higher loans for borrowers with such irregular repayment records. Instead of publicly rejecting the loan requests and diminishing the stature of the Branch Manager in front of his staff, the Area Manager took him aside. They discussed the problem, and concluded that the Branch Manager should resubmit the loan applications with recommendations for smaller loans, within the capacity of borrowers to repay.

Some managers were observed publicly chastising subordinates and clients. For them, traditional patterns of authority remained strong. One lost his temper on several occasions because of poor discipline he observed in the centers and poor record keeping at the Branch. He criticized a Bank Assistant in front of client members at a center meeting. Another Area Manager was publicly critical of a Program Officer and a Bank Assistant in a Workshop. He spoke harshly to a woman who was having difficulty answering a question. Later he explained that "sometimes you need a harsh voice so that people take you seriously." The authoritarian style of these two managers reflected behaviour traditionally expected of higher officials in the larger society. Not all Grameen managers are able to follow new role models.

Diluting the Impact of Hierarchy

Observations showed a range of hierarchical and non-hierarchical behaviors. On the part of some senior and field managers there were explicit efforts to try to demolish the barriers created by hierarchy and hierarchical behavior.

Consistent with traditional expectations, most Branch Managers offered their desk and chair to the Area Manager or Program Officer when they came to the Branch office. Some Area Managers, however, routinely insisted that the Branch Manager keep his seat; others just as naturally took over the Branch Manager's seat. In visiting centers, the first type of Area Manager would sit to the side and allow the Branch Manager or Bank Assistant to play the primary role; the second type of manager would sit in the center and take over the dominant role. Some Area Managers refused offers by subordinates to carry their motorcycle helmets or perform other personal services. Others demanded that subordinates carry the helmet and papers; or when in the office would even shout two offices away for a subordinate to bring a cigarette or match from the next room. In these cases, personal service seemed mixed with the requirements of professional service. Behaviors on the part of both the manager and the subordinate suggested that for them personal service is acceptable in a professional setting.

All managers observed, however, generally followed a routine of personally greeting and shaking hands with all staff members when visiting a Branch. Some insisted on themselves introducing the researcher/visitors; others deferred to the Branch Manager to make the introductions.

Two of the managers observed took special steps to involve women staff, or to facilitate their work. Both clearly made an effort to ask questions of women staff at formal and informal meetings in order to bring them into the discussion. One made an effort to facilitate transport to distant centers for which one female Branch Manager was responsible. (Female Branch Managers, like their male counterparts, are entitled to a bicycle. Cultural norms make it difficult for a Bangladeshi woman to ride a bicycle.) The efforts of these managers to support female staff was remarkable both in terms of the surrounding cultural expectations, but also because their own family patterns were traditional.[6]

Grameen management has not had success in creating the conditions that encourage growing numbers of women to work with Grameen. The next chapter gives some statistics illustrating the weak performance in this area. The cultural barriers, and the logistical barriers of housing and transport, make progress in increasing women staff difficult. On the other hand, senior management had not, by 1991, taken the strong measures, such as setting targets, for increasing women staff, as it did for attracting women clients. Senior management is aware of the problem and exploring ways to address it.

Overall, the data suggest variation in the way actual field manager behavior matches articulated organization values. Two factors seemed to influence the variation. Area Managers demonstrated better listening and supporting as well as non-hierarchical behavior when they developed routines that fostered those values and when they had role models of such empowering management.

Routines and Role Models

All managers observed seemed to have a routine of greeting all staff on visiting a Branch Office. Many Area Managers spoke of organizing periodic festivals or outings for Area staff as a way of fostering good staff relations. The pattern and indeed requirement of frequent visits to Branches and centers puts the managers in direct and constant contact with subordinates and clients. Individually some of the managers spoke of consciously organizing their work so that it was consultative. One manager explained that he likes to have two periods of work in his office each day at which time he likes to sit down with the Program Officer and Senior Assistant to review the mail and scheduled field work in order to develop a common approach. Another talked about purposeful efforts to establish a personal relationship with all staff in his Area. Another reviewed loan applications directly with Branch Managers so that they shared criteria for loan approvals. Others seemed more haphazard and in particular did not plan for consultation on decisions.

The managers who consciously structured consultation with staff referred to role models for their behavior among Grameen senior managers. Several referred to the consultative character of decision-making among senior managers. Another said that his style of management was the "Yunus" style and he referred to a story of when the Managing Director and General Manager were visiting Tangail. Working early in the morning, they needed something typed. When the typist came to the office, he asked Dr. Yunus if he could be excused for an hour to do something urgent in the bazaar. Dr. Yunus agreed. The General Manager was puzzled and asked why the typist was allowed to go when there was urgent typing. Dr. Yunus explained that if he had refused the man's request his mind would have been in the bazaar and not on his work. The quality of work would have suffered. It was better to allow him to solve his problem in the bazaar and return committed to his work.

The message of this "story" was not the permissiveness implicit, but the regard for the needs of the subordinate and the conditions that would enable him to work most effectively. This Area Manager also suggested that the two recent Zonal Managers in his Zone had tried to nurture the "Yunus style".

The role of Zonal Managers as management models may be important, but the limited observations of their management practices suggests that Zonal Managers' practices reflect a variety of models. Their management of zonal meetings observed indicates different conceptions of participation. One manager indicated that he does not make decisions on his own but throws issues out to a Zonal meeting for discussion. Yet in the staff meeting observed in his Zone, discussion was almost totally limited to the Area Managers; Program Officers and Zonal Office staff spoke rarely. He suggested that this was due to inexperience, and that when they became Area Managers they would participate more freely.

In another Zone, the Zonal Manager structured the discussions so that he systematically called on all meeting participants, including women staff, to comment on key issues. In another situation, a Zonal Manager structured seating at an Area staff workshop so that female Bank Assistants sat off to his side, out of eye contact, making their participation physically more difficult than for the male Bank Assistants.

Manager Time Allocation

Do managers focus their time on subordinates and clients, or are their attentions directed up the organization ladder? Time allocation is important. It sends a message about priorities. It also puts practical boundaries on the manager's capacity to manage core staff. Time spent with subordinates and clients is easily measured through simple tracking of time spent by activity and place. It captures the quantity if not the quality of managers' interactions with subordinates and clients.

Observation data suggest that the managers observed spent from nearly one quarter to nearly half of their time with subordinates and/or clients at center meetings, loan utilization and Deep Tube Well visits, and Branch offices. Bank Assistants and sometimes the Branch Manager were always at the centers, Deep Tube Wells and loan utilization sites when visited by the Area Manager being observed. Clients were at the Branch Office only for loan disbursement and generally had little contact with the Area Manager at that time.

Table 1 presents findings on time allocation patterns of six managers observed. The length of time the Area has been operating, transport logistics and other factors also affect time allocation decisions. The observed time allocation patterns do allow some tentative generalizations:

- Grameen managers work long days, between eight-and-one-half and nine-and-one-half hours. Four of the observations took place during the month of Ramadan when it was expected that fasting might shorten the work day. While not excessively long hours by some First World manager standards[7], these hours are substantially longer than hours worked by Grameen Bank manager peers in commercial banks or government.
- Grameen managers spend the largest portion of their working time with subordinates and clients: from 24% to 49% of total work time. Time spent in the Branches ranged from 15% to 33% of total

Table 1. Manager Time Allocation

	Manager					
	1	2	3	4	5	6
Average Time worked per day (hours)	9.2	8.6	8.8	8.7	9.8	8.6
Percentage of time traveling	25%	40%	40%	26%	37%	61%
Percentage of average time per day at:						
Centers	7%	12%	3%	9%	21%	13%
Monitoring loan utilization	neg.	4%	2%	2%	0	0
Branches	17%	30%	26%	33%	15%	21%
Deep Tube Wells	-	-	4%	5%	-	-
Area Office	28%	12%	23%	25%	-	7%
Zonal Office	11%	-	-	-	-	-
Other	22%	1%	2%	-	6%	-

(Source: Grameen Bank)

manager time. Additionally, the two managers with Deep Tube Well responsibilities spent respectively 5% and 4% of their time at the DTW sites. Time spent in the centers, the principal client contact, ranged from 3% to 21.5% of total manager time. Additionally, managers spent up to 4.3% of their time in checking on client utilization of loans. Grameen field managers appear to spend more time with clients than is indicated as the norm in some research on manager time allocation patterns in industrialized settings.[8]

■ Travel time consumes an enormous portion of the manager's work day. Managers devote from 25% to 61% of their time travelling to centers and Branches in their Area. To some extent the travel time reflects both the size of the Areas for which managers are responsible, as well as the limitations of the roads or other transportation infrastructure. Nonetheless, the large portion of time devoted to one function, travel, that is only a means of achieving the real objective of taking credit to the village level, suggests opportunities for introducing logistic efficiencies in time use and scheduling of manager attendance at center and group recognition meetings. The enormous differences in travel time (25 to 61% of total work time) suggests the possibility that some managers have found ways to streamline their travel.

■ The quality of manager time allocated may be affected by punctuality. It was clear from the observations that some managers are consistently late for scheduled center and other meetings. Time and lateness have different meanings in different settings. Here lateness was defined by arrival at a center when a scheduled meeting was finished or when concern over lateness, specifically or generally, was expressed by the manager or by subordinates. One Area Manager addressed his own problem of keeping to schedule in a discussion with subordinates, acknowledging the interference with work flow. Another identified the problems caused by delay to clients who may be day laborers needing to report to jobs. To the extent that managers serve as a model of disciplined behavior to clients, lateness may be a negative factor. Looking at manager time allocation in a different way, Table 2 indicates big differences among the number of minutes managers spend in village centers as opposed to Branch Banks. Two managers from one Zone spent more time in Branches than centers. They explained that they are located in one of the oldest Zones, adjacent to the capital area. The

Table 2. Manager Daily Time Allocation
By Branches and Centers Visited
and by Average Time Per Visit (in minutes)

	Manager					
	1	2	3	4	5	6
No. of Centers visited per day	1.6	2.0	1.0	1.6	3.5	4.0
Average time per visit (minutes)	25.0	30.0	18.0	32.3	36.1	31.8
Average time per day (minutes)	40.0	60.0	18.0	51.7	126.3	55.2
No. of Branches visited per day	1.3	1.3	4.0	2.0	2.2	1.5
Average time per visit (minutes)	71.0	117.5	34.3	86.8	40.3	49.0
Average time per day (minutes)	92.3	152.75	137.2	173.6	88.6	88.2

(Source: Grameen Bank)

economy is relatively strong, able to sustain enterprises capable of supporting repayments on loans larger than in other, newer Zones. This allows Branches to expand disbursements to a profitable level. The age of the Zone means that banking procedures are well established in the Branches and centers. One of the Area Managers in this older Zone explained that, because banking procedures are well established, he did not have to spend much time monitoring registers. Instead he focused on building and maintaining morale of field staff. Manager 2, who also spent more time in Branch Bank offices, was having transport problems at the time of the research. In contrast, managers in the younger Zones (three years and under) emphasized the importance of their being in the centers to build center "discipline" and habits of regular client attendance and repayment.

Conclusion

Does the management behavior of Grameen Area level managers correspond to the articulated organization values of empowering management? The data suggest a qualified "yes" answer. In a society where the cultural norms are fatalism, deference to authority and concern with status or hierarchy, Grameen has achieved a reversal of direction. It appears to be in the process of establishing its own culture of empowering management in a larger society that remains fatalistic, hierarchical, and authoritarian.

Field managers were observed welcoming experimentation and being open to change. Most showed capacity to listen to and to support subordinates and clients. Some managers explicitly attempted to discard traditional, hierarchical relationship patterns in their interaction with subordinates and with women. All managers observed followed routines or schedules that brought them into regular contact with subordinates and clients. Often there were routines that structured opportunities for staff and clients to participate in discussion and that created conditions of equality among staff. Senior staff generally offered role models of participatory and empowering management styles. Field managers identified these role models as guides to their own behavior.

Creating an organizational culture and encouraging management styles that differ from the norms of the surrounding society is difficult.

What is remarkable is that Grameen has succeeded so well. Where weaknesses exist, senior management has been prepared to identify them and to seek solutions. It has, for example, recognized weaknesses in the listening skills of field managers and developed in-service training to meet the need. It recognized the complaints of Bank Assistants and quickly met with union activists to address problems. It has acknowledged the difficulties in creating the conditions that would allow increasing numbers of women to join and stay with the Bank as field staff.

This chapter suggests that the observed management practices of Grameen, particularly at the field level, are largely, if not wholly, consistent with the values the organization has expressed. The next chapter explores how the organization instils these values in staff, and what management techniques senior management uses to sustain these values.

Notes

1. Tom Peters, **Thriving on Chaos: Handbook for Management Revolution** (New York: Harper and Row, 1987), 381.
2. Susan Davis, Interview by author, New York, May 1991.
3. Jan Moris, "The Transferability of Western Management Concepts", in Black et al., eds., **Education and Training**, 77.
4. David Abecassis, **Identity, Islam and Human Development in Rural Bangladesh** (Dhaka: University Press Ltd., 1990), 34, 36, 38, 51-56, 63.
5. Area Manager, Bhuyapur, Informal interview by author, 29 April 1991.
6. The wives of some managers, for example, led secluded lives, following a traditional practice of eating separately after the husband, family males and visitors.
7. Henry Mintzberg, **The Nature of Managerial Work** (New York, Harper and Row, 1973), 242-243.
8. **Ibid**.

6

CREATING AND SUSTAINING
MOTIVATION

"Motivation is not a question of salary."
Mushtaque Khan[1]

Why do Grameen field staff continue to perform work that requires long hours in unglamorous village settings when their level of education might entitle them to secure, office-based careers? Why is there so little corruption among Grameen staff who daily handle cash when corruption among their peers in government and private banks is thought to be common? What motivates Grameen staff to stay with jobs that require work under difficult conditions in rural areas and to remain honest? How does Grameen Bank management create and sustain their motivation to do so?

The last chapter suggested that field manager practice is remarkably consistent with articulated organization values. Field staff appear to be absorbing and adopting the organizational culture of Grameen Bank. It is a culture that differs from the surrounding traditional culture of Bangladesh society. This chapter goes on to show that Grameen has created an organization that is largely free of corruption and where there is little turnover of field staff. How does Grameen Bank inculcate the values and vision of the organization? And how does it sustain the motivation of staff to support the values and vision?

Research on the management of motivation in field or extension staff in development work has been limited, even though poverty alleviation work, which is dependent on face to face contact with poor people, relies heavily upon those field staff. It is field staff, not headquarters people, who are in direct contact with the poor. Yet the history of development efforts is replete with examples of extension staff who do not go to the field or who redirect the focus of their work from the client to their superiors.[2]

This chapter explores propositions about the management of motivation in the field-based, poverty alleviation work of Grameen Bank. Management of motivation is centralized and senior management draws on a range of tools for this function. Grameen manages the creation of motivation primarily through induction training. It sustains motivation through management of formal and informal reward and recognition systems that address a range of the survival, status, and self-actualization needs of staff. Pay, as a formal reward, is an issue for Grameen staff, but it does not appear to play a major role as a motivational factor. Management motivation strategies have overlapping and interacting effects. Figure 5 is a generalized overview of how motivation operates in Grameen Bank.[3]

This chapter will provide evidence, from Grameen's own records as well as from outside evaluations, that there is little evidence of corruption among Grameen staff and that Grameen is able to retain staff over long periods for field-based work that requires harder work under more difficult circumstances than is the case for similarly qualified staff in government and private banks. Data on staff commitment to vision and values were presented in Chapters 4 and 5.

Second, the chapter will describe the devices Grameen uses to create and sustain motivation. Data for this section come from Grameen documents, interviews with senior management, focus group discussions with Area Managers on the sources of motivation, observations of Area Managers at work and informal interviews. The data collected focus on officers, particularly Area Managers, who represent management at the operational level. Evidence about non-officers, who represent more than two thirds of Grameen field staff, is limited because of language barriers, time and other constraints on field research. This is an area where more research is needed.

Building and maintaining motivation of non-officers may be the most important, but difficult, task for Grameen management. Bank Assistants, who have daily contact with clients, are the "foot soldiers" of Bank operations. It is among the non-officers that the trade union movement tried to organize. It is among the non-officers that the tensions between staff needs for income, good working conditions and status and the organizational requirement of commitment to organizational vision and values are most clearly seen. Moreover, it is among the non-officers that Area Managers may have the greatest capacity to influence their level of motivation. Observation data suggested the possibility that where Area Managers are good listeners, supportive of their staff, and non-hierarchical in style, there is evidence of greater non-officer commitment to Grameen work (Chapter 5). Field management style itself is probably a critical motivational tool with respect to non-officers.

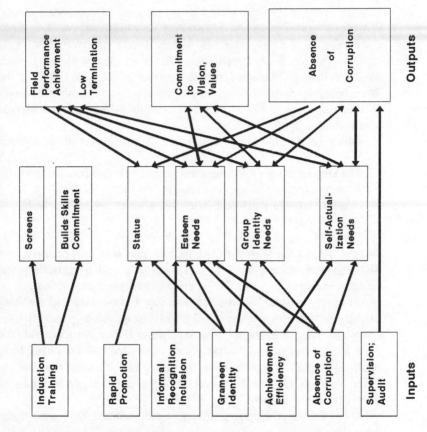

Figure 5. Dynamics of Motivation in Grameen Bank

103

Motivation

Finally, this chapter identifies some of the systems, discussed more fully in Chapters 7 and 8, that make it difficult for corruption to take place.

Corruption

Grameen has an apparent record of a low level of corruption among staff in a country where corruption is considered commonplace. Corruption is recognized at the highest levels of government as a critical obstacle to development. The then newly elected Prime Minister Begum Khaleda Zia was quoted in March 1991 on the paramount importance of stamping out corruption: "...our prime task at this time would be to build a corruption-free, people-oriented administration".[4]

Observers of rural credit have noted the prevalence of corruption:

> Throughout Bangladesh whenever people talk about credit, there is everywhere a flat opinion stated: "no bribe, no loan". It is usually expected that one has to give 10% of the loan as bribe (*gus, najrana*).[5]

One Grameen Area Manager explained the pervasiveness of corruption in Bangladesh society as a form of survival and as reflecting the primacy of family loyalty. To get a job in many places, particularly in Government, he said, it is necessary to pay a bribe. He told the story of the police officer who exacted a "toll" from passing cars, trucks, buses and even pedestrians. Asked whether it was not shameful, the Area Manager explained that the policeman had to borrow money from relatives in order to pay the bribe to get his job. He takes the "toll" to repay his loans. It would be more shameful not to repay his relatives than it is to take a bribe.

Other Grameen managers talked of the pressure they came under from their families for their failure to take bribes. Their cousins and peers may have equivalent level jobs in commercial banks for which the official salary is the same as in Grameen Bank. But their cousins and peers, taking bribes, have a larger actual income and higher consumption levels. Wives and families sometimes ask why the Grameen staff are not earning so much as their cousins, and why they travel so much and work long hours. By the prevailing social norms, Grameen staff may be considered "failures" in comparison to their commercial banking peers.

Available evidence, however, suggests that there is little corruption in Grameen Bank. There are two sources of evidence: outside evaluations of Grameen Bank and Grameen Bank records.

The Bangladesh Bank reported on an evaluation of Grameen Bank operations in 1987. An independent survey they carried out looked for incidence of corruption by asking borrowers if they paid anything for their loan in addition to a Tk.0.50 tax stamp. None of the borrowers reported paying anything additional, suggesting that at Grameen there was no evidence of bribes for loans.[6]

Grameen Bank has autonomous internal systems for identifying irregularities and corruption (see below). Md. Shahjahan, head of the Audit Department of Grameen Bank, estimates that less than one tenth of one percent of Grameen Staff are involved in corruption.[7] The most frequent opportunities for small scale corruption exist for non-officer staff, particularly the Bank Assistants involved in daily collection of loan payments and savings deposits. Abdul Razzaque, the chief of the Establishment Section, notes that unauthorized use of funds is regarded as a serious offence, and that there are very few instances of corruption. Branches are audited every 18 months with location and branches selected randomly within time eligibility for audit, and with no prior announcement of audit. When the audit suggests malfeasance or other problem, the staff member charged has recourse and an opportunity for defense. Serious offenses are subject to dismissal. The Establishment Section is responsible for disciplinary actions for officers; the Administration Department manages discipline for non-officers. Three monthly reports (early 1991) on terminations analyzed by reason for termination, job designation, posting and dates of joining and release were examined. Out of 263 terminations reported, there were only two staff terminated for corruption. This represented 0.7 percent of total terminations. The two were Bank Workers who had been with Grameen for 9 and 14 months each.[8]

Staff Retention

Table 3 shows that the longer Grameen staff work with the Bank, the less likely they are to leave employment. Seventy-six percent of terminations among Grameen Bank staff occurred among those who had

Table 3. Grameen Bank Terminations in 1990

	Staff Length of Employment				
	6 months to 1 year	1 year to 3 years	3 years to 6 years	More than 6 years	
Male Officers	122	15	1	1	
Female Officers	29	3	Nil	1	
Male Non-Officers	757	281	13	Nil	
Female Non-Officers	139	22	3	Nil	
Total	1,047	321	17	2	

(Source: Grameen Bank)

been employed between six months and one year. (The first six months of employment are spent in training and are recorded separately.) Percentages of terminations by length of employment could be a misleading statistic. In 1990 the largest staff cohort at Grameen Bank included those who had been employed for less than three years. This reflected the rapid expansion Grameen has experienced in the late 1980s. The number of officers has expanded nearly two-and-a-half times (984 to 2,323) between 1987 and 1990; the number of non-officers by more than three (3,653 to 11,303) during the same period. Terminations are nearly nil among staff employed more than three years. Either because of growing commitment to Grameen or the absence of opportunities elsewhere, once the Grameen staff pass the three year mark they are staff for life.

Creating Motivation

Induction training is a key device for inculcating norms.[9] In the case of Grameen Bank induction training goes beyond inculcating norms. It does introduce and instil the basic vision and values of the organization, but it also serves as a recruiting device to weed out new recruits who are unwilling or unable to carry out a job requiring difficult and demanding field work with the poorest people. The induction training, because it is experiential or practice based, tests the new recruit's capacity to work with the poor; brings him or her into direct contact with the poor and the causes of their poverty; and gives him or her experience with learning process and problem solving skills.

Recruitment itself is not a highly competitive process at Grameen Bank. Openings are advertised. There are educational requirements for officer candidates (master's degree) and for non-officers (higher secondary certificate). Maximum age for recruitment is 27 and, with a few exceptions where technical skills are required, there is a preference for recruits with no prior experience. Candidates with previous experience are discouraged because they may have developed bad working habits.

Candidates meeting the basic requirements are interviewed. Professor Yunus suggested that the purpose of the interview is to prepare the prospective employee for the type of field work required in Grameen so that they can screen themselves out. Interviewees are not asked whether they are committed to poverty alleviation. Instead they are told about the purposes of Grameen Bank and the conditions of training and work. Yunus explained that he was more likely to ask male candidates if they could cook and female candidates if they would ride a bicycle. In 1990, roughly 80 percent of applicants interviewed were recruited.[10]

Induction training, plus the inductees' second six months inside Grameen, when they have probationary status, play the weeding out function. In 1990 there were a total of 2,509 induction trainees of which 703 or 28% dropped out during the training. As Table 4 suggests, the dropout rate has been declining in the past three years. Overall induction training eliminates around 25 percent of male and up to 60 percent of female recruits.

The data presented on terminations (Table 3) suggested that the screening process continues at least six months past the training period. In 1990, of the 1,386 staff who terminated employment with Grameen Bank, 1,047 had been employed between 6 and 12 months, or the six month period following induction training, at the time of termination. Only a handful of these terminations were for cause, such as corruption, improper behavior or inadequate work performance.

Recruitment and retention of female staff has been a major problem for Grameen. Dropout rates are highest among female trainees, particularly among the female officer trainees. Female officers, with master's degrees, tend to come from higher status and income families; their experience may leave them less prepared and less willing to live and work under the difficulties of rural conditions. Location of work away from home discourages female candidates; lodging for single women is difficult in Bangladesh. Moreover, there are thought to be greater employment opportunities for females with a master's degree than for males with equivalent or fewer qualifications.[11]

Grameen's efforts to encourage women staff have not been as successful as those of some other NGOs in Bangladesh. A strategic problem was created with the construction of a number of Bank Branch facilities using donor assistance. The design included both banking offices and staff quarters upstairs. The quarters, designed as single sex dormitory facilities, are usually reserved for male workers who represent the largest number of staff. Female bank workers must go out in the nearby town and find housing. This is an added constraint on recruiting and maintaining female staff. Senior management is aware of the problems and committed to increasing female staff. Though accurate wastage figures are not available, an estimated drop-

Table 4. Induction Trainee Dropout Rate

	1988			1990		
	No.	Dropouts	%	No.	Dropouts	%
Officers (male)	576	214	37	297	64	23
Officers (female)	---	---	--	23	14	61
Non-Officers (male)	1,587	503	32	1,807	478	26
Non-Officers (female)	26	12	46	382	147	38
Total	2,189	729	33	2,509	703	28

(Source: Grameen Bank)

out rate of 28 percent in training and of 34 percent in the second six months of attachment to Grameen Bank suggests a very high wastage. The training investment in perhaps 50 percent or more of inductees who terminate employment can not be recouped from on-the-job performance.

How does induction training weed out the unsuited and prepare motivated staff ready to work directly with the poor of Bangladesh? Trainees are sent to the field so that they can internalize the Grameen Bank philosophy. Senior managers explicitly identify this as a weeding out period. Those who do not have the commitment for this kind of work identify themselves. Induction training is six months long, consisting of three nearly two-month-long stints at different branch banks. Induction training begins with two days orientation at the Training Institute. It continues with the three 8 week field training sessions, separated by two 7 day periods at the Training Institute and a final week there for summary, testing, and a passing out ceremony.

After the brief initial orientation, the trainees are sent to the field and instructed to report to the Branch Manager. They may get his assistance with finding housing, but they may well have to find their own housing.

The training methodology immerses inductees in a pattern of learning by questioning and doing. Each time trainees go to the field they are sent with a set of questions about the nature of poverty and about bank operations. They are asked to interview and write life histories of women borrowers who had been poor and marginal. Trainees are given an interview guide that suggests questions about early childhood and youth, family circumstances and present relationships, nature and causes of poverty, particularly in relation to key events like the War of Liberation and recurrent famine and floods, status in the village and relationship with village elders. The histories are reviewed by their co-trainees during one of the periods when they return to the Training Institute.

The intention of the peer critique, the head of the Training Institute says, is to determine if each of the trainees has truly established a rapport with the Bank member and has come to understand the nature of poverty in this person's life. If the life history is judged inadequate, the trainee will return to the field and redo it. Trainees are also required to carry out village socio-economic surveys and collect market data in order to gain first hand knowledge of the conditions of rural life and economy.

Living and working conditions for the trainees are spartan. They are separated from their home districts and forced to find living accommodation in an unfamiliar setting with fellow trainees who until recently have been strangers. Daily work requires visits to villages each day, sometimes walking 10, 20 or more kilometers in hot summer sun, or negotiating muddy pathways in monsoon torrents, returning to work the next day in sodden clothes to sit in the fragile, thatch roofed center shelters. Trainees have the certainty of salary and job, but their daily experiences otherwise bring them close to the daily reality of the clients they are to serve.

The expectation is that the trainees, through the direct experience, will develop not only an understanding of poverty, but a deep commitment to working to change that poverty. They will learn how to identify and work with the poor; how to collect data; and how to draw inferences. Trainees will be encouraged to use these skills to think independently. At the least, those who fail to develop these capacities and sympathy will resign, or will fail to pass the basic tests required after field training.[12]

The induction training also prepares the trainees for the banking work which they will do in the Branches. The training does not include lectures on concepts and procedures of banking. Instead trainees are given a set of specific questions about Grameen Bank rules and procedures. They are expected to find out about group and center organization, operation of group and loan funds, loan processing procedures, record keeping, group interaction.

Grameen leadership involved with training says that the emphasis is on understanding the social and economic milieu in which Grameen loans are given. Trainees are asked to find out the importance of discipline in a group, how to motivate a group to form or to take responsibility for loans, how to assist a group in applying for a loan or a center chief in collecting loans or how to supervise loan repayment. Trainees work along with Bank staff in performing some of the basic operations, learning by doing. Through their work in the field, observing and assisting Bank Workers and asking questions, the trainees are expected to find the answers to the questions. When they return to the Training Institute, after each two month period in the field, trainees are tested on the answers to the questions.[13]

Induction training thus seeks to immerse trainees in Grameen's vision of poverty alleviation work and its values of a learning culture approach, of questioning, of openness, and of experimenting.

Motivation

Following successful completion of training, inductees are generally assigned to a Branch Bank to take on the responsibilities of a Bank Assistant. For the first six month period they hold a probationary status, and are technically called Bank Workers. During this six months they confront the responsibilities of being a Bank Assistant. They carry out routine banking functions and play a leadership role in terms of forming new groups and centers or in motivating old ones in some of the social activities of Grameen Bank. This period, as noted above, sees a further weeding out of inductees. After the first year of employment, terminations decline markedly.

Despite high wastage rates, Grameen Bank has long regarded the investment in induction training as worthwhile. A Grameen document in 1989 said that "training has always been and still is a key element in the success of Grameen Bank. The principal task in training is to turn out motivated staff with necessary skills which make them capable of rendering banking services to Grameen Bank's clients".[14] The large induction training undertaken by Grameen Bank in the late 1980s and early 1990s has supported the rapid expansion of Grameen in terms of number of Branches and area covered. The expansion and training have been facilitated by donor support.

Grameen's heavy investment in its approach to experiential recruitment and induction training does not prove whether this approach is the most effective or efficient way of achieving its selection and motivation goals.[15] It is an approach that management believes works and one which may be becoming more efficient. There is a downward trend in the dropout rate among induction trainees. While Grameen may find it useful to experiment further with recruitment measures that screen out recruits most likely to drop out during training or the second six months of employment, it should not underestimate the role of induction training in weeding out unsuitable staff. The heavy investment in the recruitment and induction process is evidence of management priorities.

Managing Motivation

Motivation is a complicated concept about which considerable research has been done and on which there are overlapping and contradictory theories. The sources of motivation may be material and extrinsic or psychological and intrinsic and the sources may vary by the individual

112

and his or her circumstances. Motivation may be exclusively linked to fulfilment of self-interest, or motivation may spring out of altruism which is independent of self-interest. Without doubt, however, managing motivation is a function of managers.

How does Grameen Bank senior leadership manage motivation? How do they perceive the sources of motivation? What are the tools for motivation that management uses to sustain staff commitment to Grameen culture of empowering management; staff dedication to fieldwork; and staff honesty. And why are Bank officers and non officers motivated to perform to Grameen Bank standards?

In searching for answers, the research for this book sought to have Bank staff and events define the sources of motivation and tools for managing motivation that operate in Grameen Bank. Data come from structured interviews with senior managers; focus group discussions with 38 Area Managers and other officers; informal interviews at the field level with officers and a limited number of non-officer staff that asked about sources of motivation; and observations. Over and over again staff were asked informally what motivates other Grameen employees to work for Grameen Bank.[16]

The results suggest that staff are motivated by intrinsic more than extrinsic rewards, and that management uses a range of techniques to manage motivation.

- Formal reward mechanisms may have considerably less motivating impact than the variety of informal mechanisms used.
- Grameen leadership has invested in symbols, communication patterns, and organizational mythology to create a distinctive Grameen community and to engender pride in the accomplishments of the organization.
- Officers articulate greater altruism than non-officers.
- Grameen senior management combines open transactions and supportive supervision with formal procedures for identifying and punishing corruption in order to keep incidence of serious corruption to a minimum.

Sources of Motivation

Money is important to Grameen Bank staff and a source of tension in their lives, but it does not seem to be the primary determinant of performance. Status or the opportunity of rapid promotion may counterbalance the lack of income opportunity at Grameen. Staff expressed pride in or a sense of belonging to a distinctive organization functioning efficiently and largely free of the corruption that pervades organizations in Bangladesh. They said they found satisfaction in interesting work and in the possibility of contributing to lessening poverty in Bangladesh.

Officers and non-officers frequently and independently raised the issue of salary levels. Salary was a topic of conversation among themselves. Bangladesh is a very poor country and staff are aware of differences in income level in the country and on the outside. Managers noted pressures from their families to bring in more money. One manager observed that a typist working for an international non-governmental organization in Bangladesh earned more than he did. Many pointed out that Grameen staff work longer hours than their counterparts in commercial banks. Nonetheless, few staff defined salary as a critical negative motivation. They recognize that Grameen management does not control salary scales. These are fixed by law and tied to levels observed at Government commercial Banks. They indicate that opportunities for alternative work in Bangladesh are limited.[17]

The observations of field managers at work, the focus group discussions and informal interviews point to a staff perception that the opportunities for rapid promotion are much greater at Grameen than in commercial banks. This perception was expressed even by individuals who did not get promoted at the last opportunity. Most of the field research took place near the time of semi-annual promotions. Area Managers were observed consulting individually with subordinates about promotions not received.

The system does produce promotions. Of those eligible for promotion in April 1991, 59 percent were promoted. As Table 5 suggests, the highest rates of promotions occurred among non-officers, and a very high rate (67 percent) among those eligible for promotion from non-officer to officer class.

Grameen staff are not just concerned about promotions. They see the Bank as a distinctive organizational community. They have a sense of belonging to an inclusive group that has a wide and positive reputation and valued achievements. Certainly not all staff share this sense of belonging, and officers are more likely than non-officers to articulate their feelings. The field managers observed explained that

Table 5 Promotion Rate Among Eligible Staff - April 1991

Table 5. Promotion Rate Among Eligible Staff - April 1991

Post Promoted	# Qualified	# Promoted	% of Eligibles Promoted
Officers			
■ Principal officer to Sr. P.O.	3	3	100
■ Sr. Officer (S.G.) to Principal Officer	80	25	31
■ Sr. Officer to Sr. Officer (S.G.)	126	45	36
■ Officer to Sr. Officer	12	7	58
■ Sr. Assistant (S.G.) to Officer	96	63	67
Non-Officers			
■ Sr. Assistant to Sr. Assistant (S.G.)	202	152	75
■ Bank Assistant (G-2) to Sr. Assistant	379	235	62
■ Bank Assistant (G-1) to Bank Assistant. (G-2)	10	6	60
Total	908	536	59

(Source: Grameen Bank)

Source: Grameen Bank

Grameen work gave meaning or direction to their lives. Interviews with other officers and senior managers also suggest that work for Grameen provides them a distinctive identity.

The Grameen identity is reflected in the blurring of the line between professional and personal life as work functions spill over into off-duty hours. All the managers used terms like "brothers and sisters" or "family" in describing their relationship to the Bank. Living in remote rural areas, the Branch Bank is not only the work center but also the recreational center for employees. Staff are thrown together, not only as outsiders coming to work in the rural area, but as participants in shared experiences.

Individually the managers would tell stories of how they shared hardships with fellow Grameen employees and how these experiences built bonds among them and with the Bank. One officer told of opening a Branch Bank in Rangpur Zone. When he first arrived he and the other Bank employee, a Bank Assistant, were able to find only a thatch roofed hut to share. On the first night a huge rainstorm came, pouring through the roof, soaking their bedding and possessions. Later they obtained a proper building with a tin roof but lacking electricity. It served as office and residence. To save money, the Branch Manager and Bank Assistant agreed to cook together, but neither knew how to cook very well and so they had to contend with the consequences of their own lack of experience in the kitchen.

Other managers spoke of bank employees standing together against resistance in the communities, where the Bank was accused of seeking to convert poor people to Christianity. Others talked about the shared experience of knowing what poverty is really like. "Working with Grameen I saw the struggle of poor people to get one meal a day though I come home at night to enough food." Grameen staff share a knowledge of the reality of the lives of the poor, a knowledge that sets them apart from other educated people, including members of their own families who do not understand why Grameen requires honesty, long hours and postings away from the home District. Grameen staff do grumble about frustrations with pay and postings. Most also acknowledge the distinctive character of the Grameen community. They identify with and greet as members of their community any Grameen staff, even those who may be strangers.

The accomplishments of Grameen Bank give meaning to this sense of belonging. All managers observed talked about their pride in being part of a major effort to reduce poverty in Bangladesh. Area Managers in the focus group discussions talked about the satisfaction coming from knowledge of having helped poor people to change their lives. An Area Manager in Dinajpur said the "greatest happiness is finding improvement for poor people" and that once a staff member has the experience of this success it makes him want to work harder.

Some non-officers interviewed expressed a similar orientation. In a Branch in Bhuyapur Area, Bank Assistants in a group discussion said that Grameen Bank work was more interesting than commercial bank work because they could see that their work had a direct impact on people's lives. One used a metaphor of a fruit tree and how the planting and cultivation led to the continuing production of fruit.

Managers identified other sources of pride in being associated with Grameen Bank. Area Managers in the Dhaka Zone focus group discussion thought that the lack of corruption in Grameen Bank was a source of pride. In Dinajpur, the commitment of staff to completing work, not putting it off until the next day, was described as a form of motivation. Most managers observed in the field did demonstrate the practice of clearing their desks of pending papers on a daily basis. They saw their role in expediting paper as part of the efficient operation of the whole enterprise in which they take part.

In interviews, Grameen staff projected an image of the Bank as a higher level organization, operating with more efficiency, effectiveness and honesty than Government. Their pride is validated, they suggested, by the international attention directed to Grameen Bank. Many staff were aware, for example, of a U.S. television documentary (CBS Sixty Minutes) on Grameen Bank and of other films made. All managers observed told stories of their experience with international visitors who came to learn from the Grameen Bank.

Methods of Motivation

Grameen leadership uses formal mechanisms of the promotion system and in-service training as well as informal mechanisms such as communications, symbols and organizational mythology to recognize performance, build identity with the organization, and articulate and legitimize the accomplishments of individuals and the organization in helping the poor. Finally, Grameen requires openness or transparency in all transactions to prevent corruption. It uses formal systems of audit and supervision to detect corruption and formal procedures of support, charges and punishment to eliminate corruption.

Reward systems are often seen as a primary technique for inducing or rewarding desired employee behavior. Like most organizations, Grameen Bank has both formal and informal reward systems. The informal reward systems may be more significant than the formal at rewarding or recognizing organizationally preferred behavior.

The primary formal reward mechanism at Grameen is promotions. Pay, as suggested above, does not appear to operate as a significant reward system since pay scales are fixed by Government. Promotions, on the other hand, are perceived as offering faster than usual upward mobility at Grameen.

Annual Confidential Review

Do promotions reward performance of Grameen vision and values? The decisions on promotion are made centrally by a committee comprised of the Managing Director, Deputy Managing Director and General Manager. Decisions are made on the basis of an Annual Confidential Review (ACR) prepared for each staff person eligible for promotion. The ACR allows for a quantitative assessment or scoring of eligible individuals against 30 indicators in 5 categories. The ACR rankings are compared with a ranked list of candidates for promotion prepared by each Zonal Manager. The materials are assembled for the committee by the Secretary to the Bank so that the committee sees only anonymous rankings.

The individual ACR is prepared by the eligible officer's immediate supervisor, and co-signed by the next level supervisor. The ACR for a Branch Manager eligible for promotion would be prepared by the Area Manager and the whole report reviewed by the relevant Zonal Manager who would have the option to endorse or dissent from the numerical rankings and recommendation for promotion. Zonal Managers prepare a separate ranking of those eligible for promotion on the basis of their field contacts during the two to two-and-a-half-weeks of touring they do each month. Is the ACR designed to allow senior management to reward staff who practice the vision and values of the organization?

The answer must be only partly yes. The ACR format does reflect Grameen's dual concern for economic and social changes in the situation of the poor. It does less well at monitoring staff performance against the expressed values of innovation and learning, openness, listening. Most important, there is some evidence that the ACR is not perceived as a tool for rewarding specific types of performance desired by the organization, but is used as a source of manager power.

The ACR is structured in a way that would enable the immediate supervisor to review an eligible staff member on the basis of measurable performance in areas that cut across both economic and social participation impacts on poor clients. The first step in the ACR is for the eligible officer staff member to list before and after accomplishments in his present post. Categories include loans disbursed, repayment rates, number of groups and centers, number of dowryless marriages, number of sanitary latrines, number of center schools. Status of loans and banking activities reflect changes in the financial condition of members. Dowryless marriages and establishment of center schools are indicators of members' capacities to make non-traditional decisions or to support their own community institutions. This data appears on the ACR before the supervising officer does the second step of the review. The second step asks the supervisor to rank the staff member, on a scale of one to five, against 30 indicators in 5 categories. These indicators are only indirectly related to the performance data in the first step.

Moreover, the 30 indicators on which the supervisor does rank the eligible officer only partly reflect Grameen leadership values of learning process approach, openness, experimentation, and questioning. Seventeen of the categories on which an officer is ranked represent generalized professional skills:

Organization ability	*Planning and*
Office work ability	*implementation skills*
Account maintenance	*Ability to keep work pace*
& report preparation	*Interest in responsibility*
Punctuality	*Sense of responsibility*
Intelligence	*Judgement*
Professional knowledge	*Supervisory ability*
Writing ability	*Speaking ability*
Ability to carry out	*Physical work ability*
responsibilities	*Decision-making ability*

Two other categories are discipline and obedience in carrying out orders. Seven categories address human relations skills that could

119

Motivation

encompass empowering behaviors of listening and supporting:

Supervisory ability   *Leadership ability*
Attitude toward   *Attitude toward colleagues*
  subordinates   *Normal temperament*
Attitude toward   *Personality*
  superiors

Four categories seem more directly related to the vision and values of the organization: one asks about commitment to Grameen Bank goals; another asks about willingness to work overtime; two others ask for a rating on "creativity" and "problem solving".

It is difficult to determine what criteria supervisors use to rank staff on these human relations indicators, or to judge how much weight is given to vision and values indicators when supervisors complete the ACR. The ACR itself does not specify criteria for the indicators.

To explore a part of this question the 38 Area Managers participating in the focus group discussions were asked about the ACR and the criteria for definition they use in ranking a subordinate on creativity. In their responses, the Area Managers nearly all linked creativity with non-routine or "non-scheduled" work. The one exception were a few Area Managers in one zone who linked creativity to performance on banking indicators. "If one Branch Manager distributes Tk.8,000 in loans and the second disburses Tk. 80,000, then the second is more creative than the first." Another measured creativity of subordinates by comparing performance against the standard indicators on Branch performance prepared by the Zonal Office each month.

In all other cases definitions of creativity referred to problem solving initiatives or innovative social development activities. Examples offered in the discussions included those of a Branch Manager's arranging for distribution of oral rehydration salts when diarrhoea hit a community; technical or other solutions to solve problems with members' enterprises when flooding, heavy rain or other disaster occurred; identification and organization of a particularly destitute group of homeless people and initiation of loans; and experimentation with children's loans in poor communities.

Whether subordinates perceive that the ACR is recognizing creative performance is not clear from the evidence collected. One discussion question for the Area Managers at focus group meetings, as well as in informal interviews with Branch Managers, brought out the likelihood

120

that the ACR functions as a tool for promotion, but not explicitly for rewarding staff practice of Grameen vision and values.

In modern management practice, performance reviews, which is what the ACR is, are generally seen as a tool for staff development. In the generic ideal of performance review, a review, once prepared by the supervisor, is discussed with the subordinate with the intention of recognizing good performance and initiating systematic efforts to improve weaknesses. When asked on a questionnaire, none of the 38 Area Managers asked said that they shared the ACR with subordinates once it was completed. Many said that they discussed performance with subordinates on a regular basis, but not in the context of the ACR. Most seemed surprised that the ACR would be shared with subordinates.

One Branch Manager, in an informal discussion, explained that "the ACR is the most important tool of the manager because all the staff know that it is the key to advancement and that the recommendation of the Manager carries heavy weight. This is the source of Branch Manager power." In another case an Area Manager being observed gave an order to the Program Officer, reminding him that the Area Manager prepares his ACR. A Program Officer who had not been promoted so fast as peers who entered Grameen Bank at the same time noted that ratings on the ACR depended on "fate". A staff member at the Dhaka Training Institute also referred to the possibility of promotion as "fate".

That the review of subordinate performance is based on personal evaluation rather than objective criteria may be reflected in the differences between the numerical ranking scores on the ACRs and the ranking by each Zonal Manager of his twenty Branch Managers best suited for promotion. There is reportedly considerable difference between the ACR scores and the rankings of the best managers by the Zonal Managers.[18]

Both Area Managers, and Zonal Managers who review the ACRs prepared on the Branch Managers have ample opportunity to review the performance of Branch Managers and to assess trends in the monthly performance indicators against the particular situation in which they are working. Grameen Bank practice is that Area Managers will visit each Branch at least twice a month. Zonal Managers are on tour between the sixth and the twenty-fifth of each month visiting Areas and Branches. There is ample opportunity for the work of individuals to be noticed.[19] The ACR could also be used as a pro-active management tool during these tours.

Grameen also conducts in-service training chiefly to prepare staff for promotion or to adjust staff to new conditions. In 1991, the Director of Training noted that a major objective of current in-service training is building listening skills. This suggests a use of training to re-enforce an empowering management culture. The focus on listening arose out of a need identified by Zonal Managers. The in-service training follows the experiential mode used in induction training. Participants are asked if they know how much they talk and whether they listen. Training for Branch Managers involves assigning them to an Area Office where they are given the job of observing how much talking is done and how much listening is done. Then they return to the Training Institute with fellow trainees and share what they have learned.[20]

Informal Rewards and Recognition

Grameen leadership has set in place a myriad of informal communication systems that serve partly as an informal reward system, but also as a process and as an affirmation of Grameen vision and culture. The leadership has established and encouraged the use of a number of communication practices that allow field staff to communicate directly with the Managing Director and with other senior staff. The practices create the opportunity or mechanism for openness, participation and sharing. In the words of one senior manager, they "make it extremely difficult for managers not to notice someone."

Branch Managers write a monthly narrative report to the Managing Director. Up to the time that the Bank had about 400 Branches, the Managing Director would look at the individual reports. At present, a staff member is assigned to reviewing and summarizing for the Managing Director all the reports and bringing to his attention particular accomplishments or problems. Area Managers provide a weekly narrative report to the Zonal Manager and these are copied to the Managing Director. The Zonal Managers report monthly to the Managing Director, commenting on staff. Additionally, staff at all levels are encouraged to write directly to the Managing Director with new proposals and reports on accomplishments or with complaints.

Grameen publishes a house organ **Uddog**, the contents of which are written by and about Grameen staff at all levels. The articles give circulation to new ideas and recognition to individual performance. Finally, Grameen Managers, from the Managing Director and other Head Office staff to Area Managers, regularly tour field operations. The Managing Director and other senior managers will attend client or staff workshops, visit Branches and go to village centers. In the process they have the opportunity to model listening and supportive behaviors for staff and clients.

This research does not assess the degree to which staff see the open communication process as recognizing or validating their participation in the larger enterprise, and re-enforcing their practice of the vision and values of the organization. Field staff do express the belief that senior management values these communications and acts on them as appropriate. Three of the Area Managers observed independently identified **Uddog** as an important participatory communication device and an opportunity for them to present their own ideas. One Area manager had just had an article published on his suggestions for streamlining reporting forms. Field staff at several levels spoke about staff letters to the Managing Director as a common practice. One Area Manager gave many examples of the seriousness with which senior managers treat staff letters. For example, a Bank Assistant wrote to the Managing Director with a proposal for decreasing the number of collection sheets (reports) to be prepared by staff at the end of the month. He devised a new form for reporting that consolidated required information and sent it to Professor Yunus. The Head Office picked up the idea, printed samples of the new form and tested them in the field. Several of the Area Managers interviewed explicitly referred to stories about Managing Director (particularly) and other managers whose management style they profess to imitate.

These informal communication systems represent a network for implementing the leadership sanctioned values of open and bottom-up, participatory communication, and they demonstrate an open participatory process. They reflect the Grameen assumptions that all people have the capacity to contribute. In this way there is an opportunity for staff to get recognition, if not financial reward, outside the scope of the normal promotion system.

Rituals and Symbols

Grameen has also developed rituals, symbols and practices which set

Motivation

Grameen apart from outsiders. Visible signs of Grameen are the Grameen salute all staff and clients use to greet each other and the practice of opening and closing meetings with exercises and shouting of slogans. Critics of Grameen have called the salute and exercises militaristic, making comparisons with brown-shirt movements in Europe. Professor Yunus suggests that the Grameen salute and exercises may have more in common with Japanese factory practices or American organizations like the Shriners than with fascist, authoritarian organizations.

The exercises are not required at Grameen. On observation it is apparent that the exercises and slogan shouting at the beginning of meetings vary from Zone to Zone, and Area to Area. One Area Manager noted that he encouraged more rigorous exercise as a way of promoting better discipline and unity among center members. In other Areas, the practice of the exercises was very casual. Grameen staff and clients invariably greet each other using the Grameen "salute", a gesture not unlike the U.S. Army salute. It sets those associated with Grameen apart from others.

The salute in Grameen, unlike the army, is egalitarian and not based on rank. The exercises are performed not only by field staff, but by the most senior staff at meetings.

Another identifying symbol is the Grameen Bank logo. It is visible all over rural Bangladesh. A line drawing of a house on a crisply painted board is the non-verbal marker of the sites of Zonal and Area Offices, Branch Banks and most centers. It makes the presence of Grameen more visibly widespread throughout the country. Grameen has the seeming ubiquity of a McDonalds' franchise in the United States.

Information and Openness

Grameen formal management systems also serve to re-enforce pride in being associated with the Bank, and make the possibility of corruption difficult. These systems are discussed more fully in another context in Chapters 7 and 8. The systems have an important impact on motivation. Grameen has a highly developed management information system which allows managers and individual staff to track accomplishments. While the primary intent of the information is to allow managers to coordinate and control performance, regular tracking of performance indicators and widespread dissemination of performance results to most managers (and staff) allow them to base their pride in the Bank on the evidence of hard data.

Audit, supervisory and decision systems also converge to make corruption unlikely (see Chapter 7). Field staff handle money every day, but daily transactions in Grameen Bank are small. A Bank Assistant may collect only Tk.4-5,000 per day. All transactions are conducted openly with witnesses. There is weekly accounting at the Branch and an audit every 18 months to catch problems. The maximum punishment for corruption is dismissal. The amounts that Bank Assistants can steal is thought to be too small to justify risking their job.

Not only openness but shared responsibility characterize operations. Decisions on granting a loan are not made by one officer alone; the decision is dependent on a series of participants. One worker alone cannot manipulate a loan decision in a corrupt way.

Conclusion

Management of motivation is centralized in Grameen Bank, chiefly through the control over the design of induction training and through a network of informal communication practices initiated and sustained over the years by senior management. Money is not the primary source of motivation. A sense of belonging to a distinctive organizational community and a sense of satisfaction or pride in personal work and accomplishments as well as in the achievements of the Bank in alleviating poverty and in remaining corruption-free re-enforce staff commitment. The rate of promotions at Grameen is greater than that in peer organizations. This encourages employees to build careers. Grameen is able to offer quick promotions because the rapid expansion has increased the number of management positions.

Senior management's capacity to rely on induction training and informal communication and recognition systems to manage motivation is determined by the environment in which it operates. Donors have been prepared to fund the induction training that contributes to weeding out staff not suited to long term field work. With salary scales tied to Government scales and with already high operating costs relative to earnings, Grameen Bank cannot use money as a source of motivation. At the same time, high unemployment and underemployment leave

125

Motivation

potentially disgruntled Grameen staff few alternative choices.

These findings about Grameen, if not unexpected, are interesting in what they offer to managers in Government bureaucracies, whose environments share the same characteristics of fixed low wages, difficult working circumstances, and few alternative employment opportunities. Grameen staff, first of all, have a steady, basic, if not an extravagant wage. Second, to work for Grameen they are forced into a rigorous field training that requires them to experience field conditions over and over again, and which exposes them not only to the needs of clients but to the potential benefits to the clients of Grameen Bank work. Once they stay with Grameen, the rewards of keeping up the hard work are recognition for their work; being a part of a re-spected organization; and pride in professional work that achieves something good for the country. The rewards are balanced against a shortage of opportunities outside the Bank.

Notes

1. Area Manager, Joysagar, Informal interview by author, Joysagar, December 1990.
2. See, for example, David K. Leonard, **Reaching the Peasant Farmer: Organization Theory and Practice in Kenya** (Chicago: University of Chicago Press, 1977), 7, 188.
3. The design of the figure was drawn from data developed in interviews and observations.
4. **The Daily Star**, Dhaka, 24 March 1991.
5. Clarence Maloney and A.B. Sharfuddin Ahmed, **Rural Savings and Credit in Bangladesh** (Dhaka: University Press Ltd., 1988), 165.
6. Bangladesh Bank (Department of Research, Rural Development Studies Cell), **An Evaluation of Grameen Bank** (Dhaka, 1987).
7. Md. Shahjahan, Assistant General Manager, Audit, Grameen Bank, Interview by author, Dhaka, 18, 19 March 1991.
8. Abdul Razzaque, Chief, Establishment Section, Interview by author, Dhaka, 19 March 1991.
9. Henry Mintzberg, **The Structuring of Organizations** (Englewood Cliffs, N.J.: Prentice-Hall, Inc., 1979), 95-98.
10. Mohammad Yunus, Managing Director, Grameen Bank, Interview by author, Dhaka, 4 December 1991.
11. Grameen Bank Phase III Annual Review Mission, Final Report,

126

Working Paper Number 7, Dhaka, November 1990.

12. Nurjahan Begum, Director, Training Institute, Grameen Bank, Interview by author, 17 March 1991; Mozamul Huq, General Manager, Grameen Bank, Interview by author, 19 April 1991; Grameen Bank, **Preparation Report**, Phase III (1989-1992), Dhaka, 1988, 40-46.

13. Nurhajan, Interview by author, 17 March 1991; Khalid Shams, Deputy Managing Director, Grameen Bank, Interview by author, 20 March 1991.

14. Grameen Bank, **op. cit.**, 40.

15. The literature suggests that there are few demonstrably reliable methods of testing potential managerial candidates. Drucker notes his findings (in a North American setting where opportunities for change are greater) that three out of five recruits quit their first employer within the first two or three years. Peter Drucker, **Management: Tasks, Responsibilities, Practices** (New York: Harper and Row, 1974), 310-311.

16. The assumption was that respondents would have greater capacity to be objective in assessing the motivation of others than in describing the sources of their own motivation.

17. In an open market situation this could mean that the most able staff members are able to leave and find equivalent or better employment elsewhere. In fact, it is not clear that most Grameen staff have equal access to such an open employment market.

18. Mozamul Huq, General Manager, Grameen Bank, Interview by author, Dhaka, 19 April 1991. Imamis Sultan, Secretary, Grameen Bank, Interview by author, 12 December 1991.

19. Huq, Interview by author, 19 April 1991.

20. Grameen Bank, **op cit.**; Huq, Interview by author, 19 April 1991.

7

STRUCTURING AN ORGANIZATION THAT EMPOWERS

"The manager's main duty is to motivate the whole group to help her [a fellow member in difficulty]"

Area Manager, Grameen Bank

Structuring organizations and their work is an ongoing task of managers. Managers, explicitly or implicitly, make strategic and routine decisions that determine whether and how the organization fosters participation and empowers field staff.

In Grameen Bank management has structured basic operating decisions so that they are decentralized to the operating level. Participation in decision-making is diffused at the field level. Grameen has designed the jobs of field level workers and managers so that they participate in and have a responsibility for the broad range of banking responsibility. Each unit, center, Branch Bank, Area or Zone operates autonomously, though each is a part of the whole. An organizational ethic of discipline and responsibility enables the decentralization and autonomy to work. Being disciplined and responsible is a necessary part of participation and empowerment.

Structuring Decision-making

One of the key operating decisions in Grameen Bank is the decision on granting a loan. Decision-making at Grameen, or elsewhere, is not a single event. It has many parts; identification of the need for decision; framing of alternatives; recommendation; choice of action; authorizing implementation and implementation.

The principal characteristics of decision-making on general loan approval in Grameen Bank are that decision-making all takes place at the field level; that those who are at the "lowest" level in the field hierarchy in most cases may play the most significant roles in shaping the decision process; and that the Area Manager, who exercises "choice" - in that his or her action triggers loan disbursal - is in routine cases performing a pro forma function. Control over the decision on loan granting is effectively pushed down to the level of those who have responsibility for loan repayment. Thus one of the unusual characteristics of Grameen is that its clients are effectively brought inside the organization structure.

Normally only the employees of an organization are included within organizational boundaries. Clients are part of the environment. In the case of Grameen Bank, the boundary between field staff and clients is permeable; clients effectively perform some of the tasks of loan officers. They therefore become part of the hierarchy or inside organizational boundaries.

Grameen clients are called "members", not customers. They must go through an examination of their eligibility and a ceremonial recognition before they are allowed to **join** a center and have access to banking services. Clients do not just decide they want to borrow money or to save. They engage in a process that effectively **commits** them to the Grameen system before they are allowed to borrow.

The decision-making process on a general loan is broken down into many discrete steps. Participation in the process is diffused among seven different individuals or groups; the power to authorize is dependent on endorsement by multiple levels but is singularly held by the Area Manager. Those who recommend also participate in the implementation through monitoring of loan utilization and payback. Identification of loan purpose is a solo activity of the individual member. Most parts of this process take place at the client level, in the center. The key exception is the disbursement where the borrower and two witnesses come to the Branch office. The flow chart in Figure 6 depicts the general loan decision process.

The loan decision process begins with the eligible member's identification of the small business she or he wants to finance and an estimate of the capital required. Typically, a proposal is discussed within the group and at weekly center meetings which the Bank Assistant attends. The group, center and Bank Assistants may make suggestions or encourage the member, and give advice on the appropriate amount of the loan, but the selection of the enterprise rests with the member. The Bank Assistant will help the member in preparing the preliminary loan application (Form 2). The proposal is discussed in the group and the center; the group and the center must give their clearance before the Bank Assistant recommends it to the Branch Manager. If the Branch Manager agrees to the loan proposal, it is his job to prepare

Figure 6. Loan Decision Process

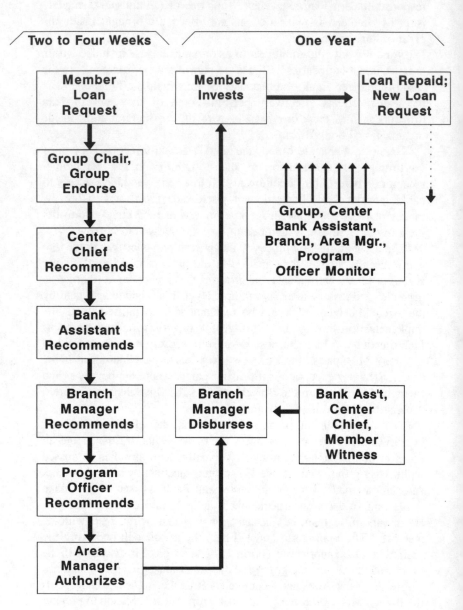

the final loan proposal (Form 2A) which is sent to the Area Office. At the Area Office, the final loan proposal is checked by the Program Officer. If the application is complete and accurately prepared, the Program Officer forwards it to the Area Officer whose signature authorizes the Branch Manager to disburse the loan.

The process, between the time the member identifies the need for a loan to Area Manager authorization may take only a few weeks. Normally the Area Manager acts on a loan proposal within a week or two of receipt, often immediately. Area Manager loan authorization in most cases observed was a routine endorsement of the recommendation of the Branch Manager. There were exceptions that required exercise of independent and professional judgement. During the observations of Area Managers at work, a few rejected proposals because of inconsistency in figures, or they delayed or altered recommendations. For example, a series of loans to Moslem clients were postponed until after the then upcoming Eid holidays. The Area Manager feared that if the loans were disbursed before the holiday the women borrowers would face irresistible pressures from family to spend the money on holiday consumption rather than investment. Another Area Manager returned a set of loan proposals to the Branch Manager, urging him to reduce loan amounts because of repayment problems among borrowers in the Branch.

On Area Manager authorization, the Branch Manager can disburse the loan. Disbursement is a participatory process. It is the only client banking activity that takes place in the Branch office, and the group chairman and the center chief must be present so that disbursement is open and transparent.

The next part of the process has a longer time period. During the year between the time the member receives the loan and the time when repayment of the loan is complete, all parties in the decision process are involved in monitoring loan utilization. The success of loan utilization underpins the member's capacity to repay the loan, the center's capacity to sustain the loan process, and Bank Assistants', Branch Managers' and Area Managers' ability to keep loan defaults below two percent.

The group chairman, the center chief and the Bank Assistant must certify that the member has used the loan for intended purposes, and the certification must be endorsed by the Branch Manager (Form 8). The group and the center, as loan guarantors and as neighbors, serve as an informal monitor. Bank Assistants attend weekly center meetings and report weekly to the Branch Manager on each center (Form 9).

While this weekly center report form is concerned primarily with attendance and banking transactions, it lists members who failed to make a weekly instalment. Failure to make weekly payments is an early warning sign of problems with loan utilization.

Program Officers and Area Managers schedule visits to centers for a variety of functions, including verbal or visual monitoring of loan utilization. Area Managers gave different estimates, ranging from 10 to 25 percent, of the number of loan utilizations they believe they are monitoring. Field managers observed spent from a negligible amount of time to 4.3 percent of total time in the field visually monitoring loan utilization. They also discussed utilization in center meeting visits. Program Officers prepare a report (Form 19) on field visits, including monitoring of utilization, which is sent to the Area Manager and Zonal Manager. The work is structured so that field managers have direct contact with field staff and clients at critical phases of the loan process. How the managers (and staff) use those contacts depends on their creativity and problem solving capacities.

All of the managers observed used occasions of center visits to introduce or encourage actions that would support viability of member enterprises. The most common type of action was geared to the activity most frequently financed by a Grameen loan: purchase of a cow for milk or fattening and sale. Conscious of the impact of animal disease or death on member capacity to repay, managers encouraged members to use veterinary services and arranged for government extension departments to provide services and/or training in animal health and vaccination to Grameen members.

Branch Managers report weekly and monthly (Form 15) on Branch activities, including the number of irregular borrowers and number of loanees in difficulty. Area Managers collate the weekly and monthly reports of the Branches they supervise and transmit them to the Zonal Office.

Responsibility for dealing with irregular payments or a potential loan default is diffused. Area Managers, Branch Managers and Bank Assistants monitor the status of loans through weekly contact with borrowers and through weekly reporting. When problems do occur, the responsibility for solving them is pushed down to the center and group levels for solution. During research for this book, 38 Area Managers participating in four focus group discussions were all asked how they would handle a situation where a woman had borrowed Tk. 3,000 only to have her husband steal it and run off. Without exception all Area Managers who participated in the ensuing discussions said they would take the problem back to the group. "...it is the whole group's responsibility to help her in such cases. The Manager's main duty is to motivate the whole group as to how they can help her...".

One Area Manager responded that just such a problem had recently occurred in his Area. Another reported a similar case, except that the husband did not flee. After beating his wife, the husband married another woman. In this case the Area Manager went to the center and asked the group members what they had done for their fellow member. He told them that they lived in the same village and that it was their duty to be aware that the woman's husband was beating her and that they should have stopped the husband at that time. The woman had been a member of the group for six years. Following discussion, the remaining four group members organized their own husbands to go to the place where the absconding husband was living. Their husbands pressured the man to return the Tk.1,800 that remained of the Tk.3,000 he had stolen, and extracted a promise from him to repay the remaining Tk.1,200.

The Area Managers, in focus group discussions and interviews, identified a number of ways in which groups could assist an individual woman borrower in times of trouble, from helping to track down an absconding husband and generating social pressure to force him to restore stolen money, to lending money from the Group Fund to enable the woman to re-start or re-structure a failing enterprise. The role of the Manager was that of helping to identify options open to the group and of facilitating what the group wanted to do.

In cases where the group cannot solve the problem, then the center takes responsibility. A special meeting of the center may be called to identify what actions can be taken that are appropriate to a particular problem of repayment. One of the Sixteen Decisions requires that when a member is in trouble, others will help her (him) out. The purpose of group or center action is not to squeeze the member but to find solutions that will make her economically solvent.

In practice, Managers do in fact appear to push problems down to the borrower-members for solution. No dramatic cases of absconding husbands were observed during the field research for this book. Area Managers were observed responding to problems at center meetings and returning the problem to the center for them to solve. The role of the Manager was that of facilitator. In two cases there was disagreement over whether a center should accept unmarried women as members. The risk of having unmarried women as members is that they will go to their husband's village on marriage, leaving behind the unpaid balance on a loan. The Area Manager led discussions of the risks, but told both centers that they must make the decision on the basis of what they knew about the prospective unmarried members.

Designing Jobs That Enable Participation and Empowerment

Field managers and staff in the Grameen system have jobs that include both variety and responsibility for the whole banking process. They are not limited to performing one small step in the Bank work; they participate in the whole process. In the technical jargon of management, job design at Grameen Bank is enlarged and enriched. This has very much to do with staff sense of participating in the work of the organization and their belief that they are empowered to contribute positively to organization goals.

The diffused participation in the different stages of the loan decision process are a simple example of the enlarged and enriched nature of jobs at the field level. Participation is not limited to one narrow step in the decision process; most participants follow a decision through nearly all its stages. In other words, the roles of each of the participants in the loan decision process are vertically enlarged. Table 6 attempts to illustrate this vertical enlargement. It suggests that participants closest to the operation - the loan itself - are involved in four out of five of the steps in the decision process. The Area Manager, at the apex of field operations, is involved with the loan decision process only after disbursement is authorized. Area Manager involvement takes him or her to the client level to monitor the use of the loan.

The design of field level jobs is also enriched horizontally in that field staff perform a wide range of functions. During the field research, Area Managers were observed performing varied managerial functions. They monitored performance; disseminated information; engaged in problem-solving and initiated solutions; distributed resources; negotiated conflicts; built motivation; served as a spokesperson for their Area or presided over workshops and meetings. Not only did they represent their Area to other parts of the organization, they were the focal point for unit contact outside the organization. While one expects manager jobs to be broad in scope, those of a Grameen manager are particularly broad and include the kinds of contact with local government and with international visitors that give

Table 6 - Distribution of Roles
General Loan Decision Process

Table 6. Distribution of Roles in the General Loan Decision Process

	Identify	Recommend	Authorize	Disburse	Implement
Member	P			P	P
Group	S	P		P	S
Center	S	P		P	S
Bank Worker	S	P		P	S
Branch Manager		P		P	S
Program Officer		P			S
Area Manager			P		S

P = Primary role;
S = Secondary role.

recognition and affirmation to the value of Grameen work. The design of work at Grameen has evolved organically and is based on experience and the needs facing the organization. Grameen Bank does not have detailed job descriptions specifying functions of field staff. The Managing Director explained that there is nothing written down about how to perform specific tasks.[1] New Bank staff learn how to perform basic banking tasks by observing experienced staff. What senior management does is give the consistent message that the object of all tasks is to reach out to the poor and to help the poor change their lives.

As Chapter 6 suggested, the prolonged and experiential induction training socializes the field staff to not one but at least three different patterns of performing the tasks in the general loan process as the trainee trains in at least three different Branch Banks with three different sets of workers and managers. The constants are the chronology of the work flow and the requirements of reporting.

Work flow and reporting requirements do tend to narrow the options and autonomy open to the staff member. Within the performance requirements embodied in the expected work flow and reporting, as well as the overall organization goal of "reaching out to the poor" lies the range of opportunity for staff control and innovation. The organization specifies the outcomes expected and the mileposts to be met; the individual can exercise autonomy in deciding how to get there. Observations of Area Managers and other field staff at work show that there is autonomy exercised, not mindless repetition of bureaucratic formulae.

There are standard responsibilities, but variation in the way they are carried out. Age of the Area may be one contingency factor influencing the variation. All Area Managers have a responsibility for monitoring loan utilization and one of the monitoring tools used is visits to centers for verbal and visual monitoring of individual loans. An Area Manager in one of the oldest Areas suggested that he monitored perhaps 10 percent of loans.[2] In one of the younger Areas, the Manager suggested he monitored 20-25 percent of loans.[3] The observation data showed that in the two oldest Areas observed the managers generally had fewer loan utilization monitoring visits per day than the younger Areas, but longer average length of each monitoring visit. When credit repayment practices are established, the need for monitoring declines.

In the two older Areas, managers also spent a smaller proportion of their time in centers than did three of the four other managers observed. When in the centers, managers in the older Areas were less likely to check the center registers that recorded attendance and repayment statistics. One explained that operations are systematized and so detailed checking is not necessary. For them, the weekly financial accounts are a more efficient indicator for tracking performance. In younger Areas, the physical checking of registers may play a symbolic more than a merely informational function; the act of checking conveys the importance placed on habits of regular member attendance and repayment, or what Grameen Bank staff call "discipline".

Personal style also appeared to influence the ways in which managers designed the execution of their tasks. In general there was a willingness to rely on recommendations of subordinates. All managers observed promptly reviewed and acted on loan proposals sent to them. Most reviewed them extremely rapidly, giving only a half a minute to each proposal. Approval seemed routine, a foregone conclusion for most proposals. One explained that he was relying on the review done by the Program Officer and on the recommendations of Bank Managers. Another said he was scanning the proposals for the obvious errors. Two liked to consult with others in the review. One met in the Branch office to discuss loan proposals with the Branch Manager before authorizing.

The way in which work is structured in Grameen Bank is through units that each contribute to the whole independently of each other. Within each unit the manager performs "enlarged" functions. Grameen management describes this form of organization as being a series of "circles within circles". "Each bigger circle tried to pass on the responsibility to the immediately next smaller circle within itself while keeping watch on each constituent smaller circle." Each level performs a wide range of functions.[4] The appeal of Grameen circle imagery is that it avoids implication of hierarchy. An alternative representation is that of triangles within triangles, easier to represent, but which also depicts the structure of autonomous units, with broad functions, progressively enfolded within one another (Figure 7). While it implies hierarchy, it also illustrates the interaction of each unit with both its internal organizational environment and the environment external to the organization, and thus the wider scope of the unit manager functions.[5] Grameen managers are responsible for the work within their triangle, and they interact with the larger triangles that encompass them. They also interact with the environment outside the triangle, for example, with local government or village leaders. One function is to take advantage of the resources outside, while protecting work inside.

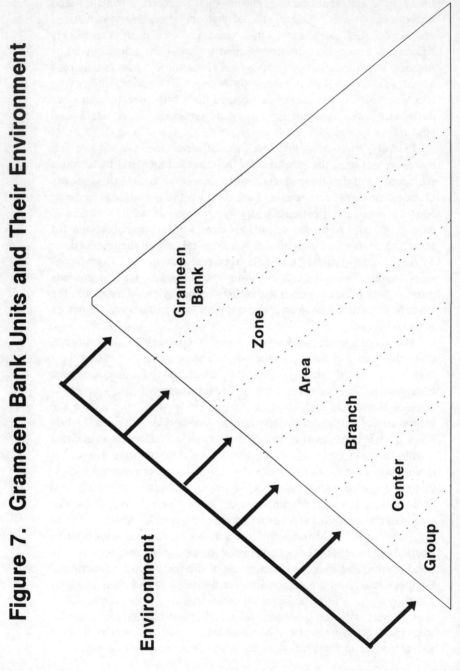

Figure 7. Grameen Bank Units and Their Environment

Discipline, Responsibility and Accountability

Decentralization of basic operating decisions as well as enriched and enlarged job designs facilitate participation and empower staff to contribute to Grameen work. Discipline is an important concept in the structuring of Grameen Bank work. The ideal and the practice of disciplined work and behavior support the viability of decentralized decision-making on basic operations like the loan decision. Discipline is the tool that enables field staff, and clients, to be responsible for loan outcomes and to be accountable.

The discipline that Area Managers, Branch Managers and Bank Assistants expect of client members is the same discipline Area Managers expect of Branch Managers in regular submission of reports and forms and in prompt management of the loan process. Branch Managers expect discipline of Bank Assistants in regular and prompt attendance at center meetings and in processing of forms and reports. The discipline modeled by staff is to be replicated in member behavior.

Discipline of the members was identified by the managers observed during the field research as a critical aspect of the loan decision process. Disciplined members were members who repaid regularly and met their obligations. Age of the Branch may influence the way in which the Area Manager tries to develop the discipline believed essential to effective loan utilization and repayment. In some of the younger Areas observed, Managers were demonstrably concerned with some of the outward manifestations of discipline. For center meetings, the members sit in six lines of five each, each line representing a group. These managers paid primary attention to whether the lines were straight; whether members were quiet and paid attention; whether women members stood up and spoke clearly and audibly; whether they performed the Grameen salute and exercises with vigor and confidence; whether members knew and could recite the Sixteen Decisions of Grameen Bank that codify the improved health, education and social practices to which members are to commit themselves.

Outsiders visiting Grameen Bank are sometimes puzzled and even offended by the attention field managers devote to seeming minutiae like the Grameen salute, shouting of slogans or whether members sit in straight lines at center meetings. To understand why these minutiae are important, it is useful to pause and consider the relationships among these outward manifestations, the integrity of the loan process and decentralized decision-making.

Structuring An Organization

Grameen Bank clients not only come from the poorest strata of rural society, they come from a class subservient to richer more powerful groups in the community. It is a class that lacks conviction that it can influence or control events in their lives. This is particularly true for the women who number more than 90 percent of the total of clients. Women have traditionally been subject to the will of men and confined to the household. They have had little expectation of being able to make decisions that can alter their lives. Poverty may have opened the doors of their houses and allowed women clients to become borrowers, but it did not automatically give them the self confidence to take their places as equals in society. In the intervention model of Grameen Bank, discipline is manifested by regular attendance, vigorous participation in exercises and slogan shouting, ability to talk to a male Bank staff member, and growing self-confidence. When women attend and participate in center meetings regularly they are saving and repaying loans regularly. In this way discipline also supports the viability of the loan decision process.

Therefore in the younger Areas, the managers are visibly concerned with "discipline" and show innovation in introducing their own methods of enhancing this discipline. One Area Manager introduced a method of rotating seating of groups so that each Group would regularly sit near the front and members be obliged to speak and participate. (This is in addition to the Grameen rule of annual rotation of group and center leadership.) Others introduced new slogans or new exercises that distinguished patterns in their Area from others.

In the older, longer-established Areas, concern about discipline was different. There appeared to be less concern about the length and the performance of exercises and slogans. One of the Area Managers explained his theory about discipline. At first great efforts are made to build member discipline in the centers. After 3 or 4 years of borrowing, members begin to take Grameen Bank for granted and there is a danger of discipline declining. This is usually reflected in irregularity of loan payments and center meeting attendance. He referred to the repayment problems being experienced in a neighboring, "middle age" Zone. Then, he said, after 7 or 8 years, "members begin to understand the importance of regular payment, of what discipline means." Concentration of Area Managers on discipline questions is no longer necessary.[6] Chapter 8 will return to the role of discipline in Grameen work and its role in building responsibility and assuring accountability, for field staff and clients.

140

Conclusion

Decision-making on routine operations is decentralized to the operating level in Grameen Bank. Participation in and responsibility for the process are diffused. The nature of this diffusion is that staff involved in the decision process participate in more than one step of the process. This implies a vertical enlargement of the job. Staff are able to follow a particular activity from beginning to end. In the case of Grameen Bank, the involvement of staff in the recommendation as well as the implementation steps of loan decision-making puts staff in a position of being responsible for the outcome of what they recommend. Within the routine flow of work, the individual Bank staff have autonomy to influence the process. Each loan is unique, varying by the member, the center, the Branch and other circumstances. Each may require slight adaptation of approach, requiring the staff member to tailor his or her approach to the situation.

In Grameen Bank, the intervention model of small scale loans to individuals with group responsibility for repayment, provides field managers the tools, the responsibility for basic operating decisions, and the possibility of participating in achieving organization goals. The loan process sets the boundaries of the operating manager or staff scope for action. Within those boundaries field staff can decide how they will deliver the inputs and how they will achieve the outputs. If empowerment means being taken seriously, Grameen field managers, staff and clients are taken seriously.

Being taken seriously also means being held accountable. The next chapter explores the meaning of accountability in Grameen Bank.

Notes

1. Mohammad Yunus, Managing Director, Interviews by author, 4 December 1990, 24 March and 1 May 1991.
2. Aminul Islam, Area Manager, Bhuyapur, Interviews by author, 27, 28, 29, 30 April 1991.
3. Abdullah, S.M., Area Manager, Dinajpur, Interviews by author, 9, 10, 11 April 1991.
4. Grameen Bank, **Preparation Report Phase III** (Dhaka: Grameen Bank, 1988), 10.
5. The Triangle device is adapted from Henry Mintzberg, **The Nature**

of Managerial Work (New York: Harper and Row, 1975).
6. Aminul Islam, Area Manager, Bhuyapur, Interview by author, 29 April 1991.

8

PLANNING AND CONTROLLING THAT EMPOWER

Accountability is an ongoing concern of development professionals. This is particularly so for poverty alleviation organizations where there are no standard models of what works. There is a tension between accountability for inputs and accountability for results. Were project inputs implemented as planned? Did the development project make a difference in the lives of poor people? There is also a tension among accountability to donors, to government, to the implementing bureaucracy and to poor people.

Grameen Bank faces these tensions and it resolves them through diffused and decentralized planning and control and information systems. It monitors and regulates performance using simple, practical indicators that capture both accountability for inputs and for results. Grameen uses targets for performance, but its senior management does not allow focus on short term targets to distort its central mission of changing the lives of poor people.

Planning and control systems, supported by information systems, are generic ways of assuring accountability.[1] Grameen Bank, as described below, relies on a performance control system that involves staff at all levels in planning, monitoring, implementing and making corrections to keep performance on track.

At Grameen performance plans first of all provide a set of goals and a road map. Second, the performance control system provides the framework for monitoring (measuring) and regulating performance according to the plan. Third, information systems generate regular and timely information that managers use to adjust implementation. Finally performance controls are used as a motivational device to spur performance. Participation in setting performance goals (management by objectives), free access to information on performance, and support to making adjustments build commitment.

Grameen's performance planning and information systems are rooted in its organizational vision and values. Grameen has given its managers and workers a clear task, that of supporting "disciplined" borrowers/members. Quality for Grameen is serving the poor not just by making loans, but by helping members become regular repayers or good borrowers.[2] Grameen's product is not simply credit delivered to poor people. It is also the creation of a client organization in the centers that encourages repayment and increasing capacity to use credit. The product of client organization and regular repayment also assures accountability for Grameen inputs, and allows them to maintain a 98 percent repayment rate. In Grameen a convergence among responsiveness to poor clients with credit, group responsibility and center discipline and accountability for loan funds is built into operations. Center discipline and group responsibility assure the repayment of loan funds and the viability of the whole operation.

Performance Control

The planning and control system in Grameen Bank is a performance planning model. This chapter suggests that

- Grameen staff at the operating level rely principally on two measures of quality credit operations: client repayment and center meeting attendance.
- Grameen has in place formal and informal information systems that provide rapid feedback on performance and are used to support management of performance.
- Grameen Bank manages the tension between its poverty alleviation and its commercial viability goals by bifurcating responsibility. The responsibility of field staff is the quality (discipline) of the center operations. The macro-issues of profitability and sustainability remain a senior management responsibility. The two levels of responsibility work together like the thumb and index finger.

Planning performance objectives, monitoring their achievement, and controlling or regulating implementation are individual functions that may be separated for analysis. In fact the three functions interact with each other. Goals may be set, but monitoring and communicating performance achievements and regulating implementation can serve to reshape the original goals.

In Grameen Bank it is particularly interesting to watch this interaction, and how management appears to attempt to control the inherent tension between its financial or banking objectives that are easily measured, and its social and empowerment objectives that are less easily defined and measured.

Annual Budget and the Five Year Plan

The major organizational planning tools in Grameen Bank are the annual budget plan and the five year plan. The annual budget focuses on financial planning, but includes plans for social activities. The five year plan is primarily a financial tool and is designed as a flexible, rolling process. Within a framework of Head Office provided formats, planning is a process that begins at the operating level, with plans and projections adjusted and aggregated as they move up the hierarchy to become an organization plan. The financial planning is increasingly dependent, at Head Office, Zonal and operational levels, on a computer based information or monitoring and evaluation system (see below). The information system provides senior management with the system-wide data to develop techniques (model branches, branch scores) that begin to allow them to project expected performance into the future and to manage financial resources more effectively. It also allows for the rapid collection and analysis of information on both banking and social activities and return of this data to operating managers in ways that allow them to follow trends and make comparisons with performance of other units.

Budgeting and planning are intertwined. The budget is prepared by August of each year and lays out the financial plan for the coming year. It projects all income and expenditure by budget category and line for the coming year, by quarters. It also includes the current budget, actual performance against budget during the first six months of the current year, plus revisions for the remainder of the year. It also reviews and projects profit position.

In the same way, the Annual Plan forecasts financial and social activities for the coming period. Key financial actions include projection of loan disbursements, loan collections, deposit and savings positions, income, expenditures and profit/loss position. These are covered in about 50 separate lines. Projection of social activities (e.g. water purifier distribution, workshops, center schools, marriages without dowry) occupy about 15 lines. Numbers of members, groups and centers, as well as staff requirements are also projected. Projec-

Figure 8. Flow of Budgeting and Planning

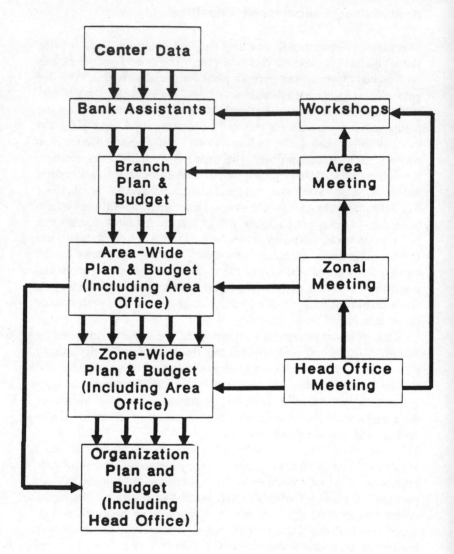

tions are accompanied by the plan for the current year, actual performance during the first six months, and revisions to the current plan.

The Five Year Plan is a projection for each of the five years for income, expenditure and profit/loss. It also projects personnel requirements, numbers of members and loan disbursements and collections. It does not project requirements for social programs.

Planning and budgeting activities are coordinated through the Planning Department in the Head Office. It has developed fairly explicit guidelines on how different lines in the budget and plans are to be determined or calculated. While certain budget items are to be calculated on the basis of fixed rates (interest income, depreciation) and others on the basis of past trends (rental or other expenses), some lines are to be determined on the basis of discussions between officers and Bank Assistants, and clients. For example, estimates of numbers of members or the amount of loans to be disbursed in the coming year are explicitly to be decided by officers and workers together. The design of social programs and specification of inputs (seeds, plants and other materials required by members) are dependent on the number of members. The number of members depends not only on the efforts of the Bank Assistant, but also on the capacity of groups and centers to expand. Estimates of members and social inputs therefore need to be based on discussions with members as well. A model of the budget and planning process is described in the flow chart below.

Planning and budgeting begin in the Branch with discussions at the center and the Branch. Figure 8 depicts (in a simplified manner) the flow of planning and budgeting. On the basis of discussions and review of trends and past experience with staff, the Branch Manager prepares the annual budget and plan, and updates the five year plan on forms provided by the Head Office. These are submitted in draft form to the Area Office and may be revised by the Area Officer based on his assessment of the Branch estimates before they are aggregated into an Area Plan and sent to the Zonal Office where the draft is again reviewed and aggregated before being sent to the Head Office.

This review process may be direct or iterative, depending on circumstances. The Head Office may also revise plans on the basis of its assessment before developing the organization plan. Once approved, the organization plan is disaggregated to Zonal budgets and plans, which are then sent back down the hierarchy. During the planning process, there may be discussion across levels of the hierarchy. For example, a Zonal Manager may run a workshop for Bank Assistants to

147

discuss planning or budgeting requirements.[3]

During implementation of the budget, quarterly reports on performance against plan are prepared at the Branch level and then aggregated up the hierarchy. Figure 9 suggests the process. The Zonal Office, working through the Area Managers, carries responsibility for budget monitoring and for action when performance differs from plan.

The structuring of the planning and budgeting process gives emphasis to Grameen Bank's role as a bank rather than its social functions. As noted above, the preponderance of lines in the budget and plans (which are really financial plans) refer to banking operations, not social activities. The narrative questions that must be answered as part of the budget and the five year plan all relate to banking operations.

Sophisticated Planning Tools

Indeed the definition of planning in Grameen guidelines suggests that planning or forecasting is essential to successful running of the Branches. The consortium of donors supporting Grameen Bank expansion during the 1989 to 1992 period urged more rigorous financial planning methodologies on the Bank both to help Branch Managers reach profitability at a faster rate and to manage funds in the most efficient manner. The 1990 Annual Appraisal team worked with Grameen staff to develop a model of a typical well-performing branch and to use it to predict future volumes of new savings and loans. The appraisal mission argued for the efficiency of a good model in prediction because it is able to incorporate more variables (such as age of Branch, age of members, loan amounts of members of differing ages) than is the traditional methodology of tracking trends in loan and savings volumes. This capacity to predict growth accurately, both as a planning and as a motivational tool, is important because growth in general and collective loans and in savings correlate positively with the speed of a branch in reaching the break-even or profit level. Branch profitability contributes to the sustainability of the credit enterprise, and reinforces the empowerment message.

In addition to the model branch methodology, the 1990 Annual Review Mission also suggested the use of existing data to develop a Branch Manager "score" that should compare the effectiveness of Branch Managers in achieving high membership levels, and high levels

Figure 9. Budget Monitoring Quarterly Reports:
Performance Against Estimates

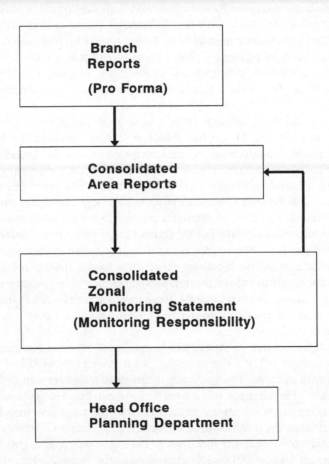

of general and collective loans in a short period. Both these character-istics have been identified as critical elements of Branch profitability.[4] Both the model branch methodology and Branch Manager scores are centralized financial planning and management techniques made possible by an increasingly sophisticated information system.

Focus on the Client In the Field

While the Grameen Bank has worked with the Appraisal Mission and others to develop sophisticated financial planning and management techniques, senior management interpretation of planning is broader than financial planning. Senior management tempers the influence of these potentially powerful, and centralizing, planning techniques with a concern for clients - a concern that permeates the organizational cul-ture.

Mohammed Mortuza, Deputy General Manager for Monitoring and Evaluation, and Masud Isa, Assistant General Manager for Planning, stress the significance of the client dimension in Grameen Bank planning. Both acknowledge that the model branch represents the goal that a branch can become profitable within six to seven years. They say, however, that Grameen's poverty alleviation mission is paramount. If branches achieve profitability but fail to improve the lives of poor people, then they have failed. In poor areas with limited resources and markets, Branches are not going to be profitable in the mediumterm. In these areas, to set plans based on a model Branch may pressure Branch staff to expand more rapidly than members can earn to repay. This means, however, that the Bank must support Branches that are not profitable through a longer period. This it can do only with outside support.

One function of planning is to determine what the consequences of expansion will be. For example, can planning help predict the rate of growth of an Area and whether it can sustain that growth, and at what rate? The strength of Grameen, Mortuza and Isa indicate, is that planning comes from the Branch; Branch staff are able to collect and assimilate local information necessary to planning objectives that are achievable. Planning functions at the organization or macro level are seen to support and protect operations at the Branch level.

Mortuza referred to several organization-wide planning require-ments: estimating the capacity of profitable branches to support the slower developing branches; planning vertical expansion of Bank activities so that credit enables the poor to move into increasingly larger, technically more sophisticated enterprises. Isa noted the use of the budget planning process since 1989 to control costs by setting limits on administrative expenditures. Both say that the Bank needs a long range planning perspective that focuses on maintaining the sustainability of banking operations whether or not the Bank continues to expand.[5]

Though planning may be structured to begin at the Branch level, it is a planning exercise that is bounded not only by the format of planning documents (as discussed above) but also by norms or expectations of what can be done. The manager of Bogra Zone referred to workshops he held with Bank Assistants as planning exercises. It was an opportunity for Bank Assistants to discuss what they could do for the betterment of their branch in the coming year. How many new groups can they form; how many sanitary latrines can they support? The Branch Manager and the Bank Assistants would set the plan for the next year, but the Zonal Manager set the parameters for planning.[6]

A Bank Assistant can normally form two but not more than four groups in a month; a Branch could organize up to ten centers in a year. It is expected that a Branch will form 100 groups its first year; 200 during the second, and 300 the third year.

In Grameen, setting objectives and planning at the operating level take place in a framework or defined environment. Structuring the planning process eliminates uncertainty and enables senior management to control the process while engaging the operators. As the Head of Grameen Bank Audit Department described it "...the strategy comes from below on how to meet the standards set from above".[7]

At the operating level managers see planning both as a periodic work function and as a necessity for the future development of the Bank. Some Area Managers suggest that the planning system is still being introduced and that they are still gaining experience with it. In general they express a high regard for the process: "If there is no such thing, how shall we advance?" "It gives us a basis to work out where we are going."

Collecting Information for Management

Grameen has avoided the management information system trap into which many organizations fall. Frequently organizations invest time

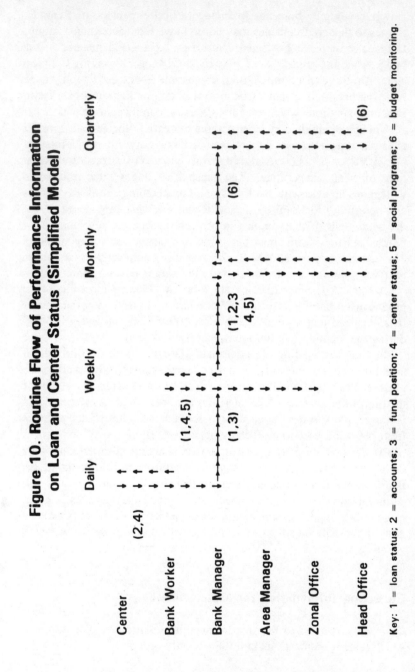

Figure 10. Routine Flow of Performance Information on Loan and Center Status (Simplified Model)

Key: 1 = loan status; 2 = accounts; 3 = fund position; 4 = center status; 5 = social programs; 6 = budget monitoring.

other resources in developing management information systems that are data-driven rather than action-oriented. The systems generate data but provide little feedback of timely information for management. These top - down approaches usually garner little support from the field staff expected to generate the data.

Grameen puts emphasis on using information, sharing information and on getting information from several sources. Because managers find the information a valuable commodity, they have a vested interest in maintaining high quality systems for generating information.

Grameen has a wide range of formal and informal monitoring systems that can be used to track performance against plan. The formal systems are a mirror of the budget and planning documents. The informal systems focus on situational aspects of performance, and on performance of social activities. Understanding the indicators of performance measured, and how they are measured and communicated, is a prelude to understanding how information is used to control performance in Grameen Bank. Figure 9 depicts a simplified model of the substance and flows of formal performance information in Grameen Bank. It may be a useful reference point in the following discussion.

Disentangling the numerous reporting forms (more than one hundred), records and ledgers and extracting the essentials of what performance is being monitored is difficult. Branch Banks seem to the outsider (though not to the insider) awash in paper and forms. Many times during the field work Bank staff were asked about the volume of paperwork and whether it seemed excessive. Without exception they seemed surprised by the question. "It's necessary, it's necessary. Is it a burden? Necessary things are not a burden." Paperwork is common in bureaucracies in Bangladesh. What is significant about Grameen is that forms are analyzed and used, and information is fed back to the operating level.

One needs to see all the paper and reporting in two perspectives. First it generates information for decision-making. Second, it tends to structure the daily work of operational staff. The model in Figure 10 simplifies the reality of "hard" quantified performance measures; it does not capture the qualitative performance information collected; it does convey some of the answers to the following questions:

- What performance indicators are measured?
- How often are indicators measured?
- Who gets the measurements and when?
- How is the information used?

Planning and Controlling

Tracking Performance Indicators

Quantitative data are collected on five key sets of performance indicators: disbursements and collections; fund position; basic accounts; status of center operations; and social program performance. The first set concerns the status of loans disbursed, collections and rates of repayments.

The second set has to do with the fund position of each Branch; tracking cash in hand, on deposit at the local commercial bank and committed to loans. It is a measure of the efficiency of each Branch in using the funds available to it. Together these sets of indicators track the income position of the Branch. These indicators are tracked daily (by the Bank Assistants and the Branch Manager) and are reported on a bi-weekly level to the Area Office; and from there on a weekly level to the Zonal Office. They are also reported by each Branch in a monthly statement (Form 15). Form 15 also includes 18 lines for reporting by gender on accomplishments of special programs (e.g. number of seeds, poultry, saplings distributed; center schools organized). A copy of Form 15 is sent to the Area Office and the data from Form 15 is entered into the computer at the Zonal level and sent on (in diskette form) to the Head Office.

The third set of indicators are accounting measures that track income and expenditures. It duplicates some of the information in the forms above on collections, interest earned and deposits, but its focus is to provide an income and expenditure statement that allows tracking adherence to the planned budget and a picture of assets and liabilities. The Branch keeps income and expenditure ledgers on a daily basis. Monthly statements (Form 35) are sent to the Zonal Office for amalgamation and transmittal to Head Office. Area Offices, Zonal Offices and other units in Grameen Bank also prepare Form 15 and other key forms. Form 35 was designed by the Accounts Department in the Head Office and serves as the tool for monitoring the budget.

Related to accounting information is administrative data collected. Information on number of employees, particularly on number of Bank Assistants by number of groups they serve, allows the calculation of a Bank Assistant utilization ratio or a measure of the relative efficiency of each Branch Bank.

The fourth set of indicators track operations at the center level through reporting on meeting attendance and repayment rates. Bank Assistants record information on a daily basis in center registers and in ledgers on attendance. They amalgamate the information on a weekly basis in Form 9, Weekly Center Meeting Fact Sheet, which is prepared for the Branch Manager. Center members themselves participate in monitoring, particularly through Form 8 that documents loan utilization of members. Center Chiefs validate this form with their signature. Branch Managers report weekly on center attendance and repayment rates to the Area Managers, who transmit that information to the Zonal Office in a Weekly Statement of Center Meetings.

The fifth set of indicators are measures of progress on social programs. Bank Assistants provide a weekly statement on social programs and these are, as noted above, consolidated by the Area manager into Form 15 for transmittal to the Zonal Office and to the Head Office.

Apart from these five key performance indicators, there are other formal monitoring systems. A key one is the Audit system described on page 105. Audit teams independently verify accountability of fund use from the center level upwards. While they have an open mandate to audit management performance, their priority at the branch level is to verify loan utilization and repayment. The reports on audit results bypass levels in the organization structure and are reported directly to Head Office where executive summaries are prepared for the Managing Director.[8]

Using Informal Information

There are countless forms of informal monitoring and information gathering in Grameen Bank. Most of the information is qualitative; only some of it is written and distributed. Branch Managers write monthly narrative reports to the Managing Director; the Area Managers write weekly reports with copies to the Managing Director. These narrative reports are not compulsory, but managers interviewed insist that most managers send them.

All staff are invited to write directly to the Managing Director or other Head Office staff. These letters are more than a one way form of communication. A special unit in the Managing Director's office summarizes major issues raised in the letters and reports. Problems are referred to Head Office or Zonal Office managers for solution. When questioned informally, Area and Branch Managers expressed the belief that their reports are taken seriously. Several told stories of responses they received. One told of a nine page letter from the Head of the Monitoring and Evaluation Unit at the Head Office. The Area Manager had written asking why the Bank did not just remove members who were not making regular repayment. The response, the Area Manager said, was that Grameen Bank operates not just to make loans, but to make good borrowers out of the poor.

Informal communication mechanisms enable simultaneous up - down communication. Staff workshops are common in the Zones and Areas, and give managers an opportunity to question subordinates on operations and conditions. They also give subordinates a real opportunity to raise their own concerns.

Tours and visits to centers, Branches and other facilities are integral to the schedules of all Grameen Bank Managers. Branch Managers, Area Managers, Zonal Managers have scheduled tours each month that bring them into contact with members and Bank Assistants in the field. Head Office staff, including the Managing Director, tour regularly, visiting centers, Branches and Areas. The Managing Director tries to spend a week each year in each of the zones (nine at the time of the research) and will sit down with all Bank Assistants in a meeting. The tradition of Grameen is that all staff may raise issues or questions anonymously in written form prior to the meeting for discussion by the senior officer.

Trainees (in both induction and in-service training) write reports following field training that provide a wealth of qualitative detail on what is happening at the operational level. Staff of the Training Institute distil the major issues rising out of these trainee reports and relay them on to senior management. Much of the information received informally seems to serve the purpose of confirming or validating information received from formal sources, or of identifying the nature of management problems.

For example, informal reports on the listening skills of Grameen Managers and the impact of listening on morale of field staff led to starting in-service training for managers on listening skills. During training, managers are sent to the field with the assignment to observe how much listening and how much talking occurs. Following the field experience they return to the Training Institute in Dhaka and share the findings of their field experience.

Besides serving a training function, the reporting provides a general flow of information from different observers.[9] Information related to performance also flows informally in ways that might be termed gossip:

a peon or driver telling a senior manager about human relation problems of a field manager; or about the organizing activities of the trade union.

Information: A Two-Way Flow

Formal information does not merely flow upward; information is synthesized at the Head Office and sent back down the hierarchy through formal and informal mechanisms. Formal dissemination of information reflects the pattern of information formally collected. The Monitoring and Evaluation Department at the Head Office monthly sends back to the Zonal Offices on diskette cumulative information on the loan disbursements and repayment, on the savings rate and the progress on implementing special programs that was reported on Form 15. The Accounts Department on a quarterly basis prepares reports on income and expenditure and the profit position; this information, however, is not sent down the hierarchy but is prepared for senior management for decision-making purposes.

At the Zonal level rests responsibility for sending performance information down the line. Most Zones, relying on their computer capacity, develop monthly statements of **comparative data** on Areas and Branches within the Zone and covering performance in loan disbursement, recovery data, numbers of new members and groups, center formation, data on special programs and on budget. This data can be broken down by Branch and sent to each Area Manager as a comparative statement of Branch performance within his Area. Zones can also tailor reports to focus on specific Zonal concerns such as data on bank staff utilization ratios. Generally, the Zonal Office prepares monthly statements on performance (disbursements, recovery, special programs) broken down by Area for discussion at the regular monthly Zonal Meeting of Area Officers and their Program Officers. The information is also broken down by Branch and provided to Area Managers for their monthly meetings of Branch Managers.

Audit results are transmitted down the line to the Branch being audited with a copy to the Zonal Office. The Area Manager must go to the Branch in order to see the Audit results and participate in responding to any questions or problems raised in the Audit.

Of the information that comes down the line, which information is used and how it is used influences what performance is controlled or regulated. In Grameen Bank, as we have seen, the bulk of the information collected concerns loan disbursements and repayments (Form 15) plus income/expenditure and profitability (Form 35). Information on members, center attendance and special programs is collected but such data are limited to less than 10 percent of the entries on Forms 15 and 35, which are the principal sources of data. Information passed back down the line from Head Office is the consolidated information from Form 15 that focuses on disbursements and repayment, and to a lesser extent to special programs. Zonal Reports to Area Managers, as well as Area Manager reports to Branch Managers, largely reflect the data from Form 15, with variations by Zone.

Monitoring and Evaluation Units in each Zone can and do prepare computer printouts on budget items such as expenditure on travel costs, electricity, stationery by Area and Branch as well as on fund utilization. The performance data available is biased toward banking performance indicators, with some information on special programs. The data on budget performance submitted on Form 35 to the Accounts Department is not fed back through the Zonal Office but Zonal offices do disseminate this information from their own database. In 1990 and 1991, data from Form 35 were not yet entered into the computer at Head Office. Accounts were reconciled and balanced by hand.

Using Information for Management

How is this available data used as a management tool to regulate performance? Interviews with Area Managers, attendance at Zonal and Branch meetings and observations suggest that managers are given autonomy on how to use performance data. Zonal Managers make available performance data and discuss them in Zonal Meetings in the context of performance goals. Faced with multiple and sometimes dissonant goals, the Area managers seek balance between banking objectives and social goals; between quantity of loans disbursed and quality of loans by focusing on what they define as indicators of center "discipline".

The senior management perspective is to provide all sorts of **comparative** information to managers in the field, and allow them to make comparisons of their own versus the performance of other managers. Intrinsic differences among Areas make direct comparisons difficult. Grameen General Manager Mozamul Huq stressed that "the point is for Area managers to look at the figures and see if they feel comfortable".[10]   As noted above, the amount of general loans disbursed and number of members were positively correlated with Branch profitability. From the perspective of senior managers interviewed, what is important is not the figures themselves, but the trend they indicate. It is not the total amount of loan disbursement, but the trend over time. "Is disbursement going up or down?" The Deputy General Manager for Central Accounts, Zubairul Huq, suggests that Area Managers are not very much aware of financial viability issues. The framework within which they operate focuses on loans, repayment and the impact on individual members. Managers operate within a narrow framework and must balance the quantity with the quality of loans.[11]

At the Zonal Meetings attended, performance information was generally distributed in written form for Area Managers, including disbursement and repayment information on different types of loans as well as on special programs. In one Zone there was discussion of a problem in trends of loan disbursements. Disbursements were lower than they had been in the same period of the previous year. The Zonal data distributed at the meeting showed that there was a wide variation among the Areas in the amount of loans distributed in the period under review. The Zonal Manager expressed concern that disbursement be raised to the levels of the previous year and used the meetings to motivate Area Managers in lower performing areas.

Area Managers appeared aware of Branch profitability issues, level of Branch income and expenditures against what was budgeted, and trends in loan disbursement and expansion. Some managers acknowledged a competition with their fellow Area Managers on the indicators for which performance data by Area was distributed each month at the Zonal meeting. One Area Manager spoke of having no loan defaults in his Area. Another noted that six out of eight of his Branches were profitable. Most talked about the need to keep expanding membership and disbursements. "The test of a good Branch", one Area manager said, "is how much they disburse and whether the collection is timely". References to the importance of increasing disbursement levels were linked to the need to move carefully, no faster than the capacity of the Branch to make quality loans.

Ultimately it is up to the Branches to take the initiative and to determine their own rate of disbursement.[12]

This Area Manager referred to the problem in a neighboring Zone where the Zonal Manager was said to have given an order to the Branches to increase disbursement of loans. They did and the rate of loan defaults increased to 12 percent. The purpose of Grameen Bank, several Managers suggested, was not simply to extend loans and to make a profit for the Bank, it was to help members become good repayers, good borrowers. Sometimes this meant restraining the rate of lending.

Area Managers identified other financial indicators of performance they used in supervision of Branches. One Area Manager whose Area had several profitable Branches because of technology loans (e.g. loans to a Grameen Bank Fish Farm) was concerned with keeping costs down as part of maintaining profitability. Two managers observed said that their record in keeping deposits in commercial banks at a low level was a mark of their success in expanding loans and making efficient use of capital. Capital should never sit idle. Several referred to the Branch performance against the annual plan, Branch utilization of staff and trends in disbursement, repayment and other measures as indicators they looked for in supervising Branches.

In practice, straight financial indicators do not appear to dominate Area Managers' approach to supervising or controlling performance. When asked what indicators they used to assess the performance of Branches in their Areas, and when their actual monitoring was observed, Area Managers appeared to be more concerned about what they called "discipline" or more specifically "center discipline", than they were with rates of loan disbursement.

In terms of performance indicators, discipline seemed to mean five things to the Area Managers: center discipline in terms of member attendance at meetings and proper meeting conduct; proper loan utilization (invested in activities productive enough to enable repayment); regular loan repayment; successful implementation of special programs (or the Sixteen Decisions), and concentration of staff work on the centers.

Repayment rates can be tracked by Managers without going to the field, through the daily reports of the Bank Assistants and the bi-weekly reports submitted by the Branch Managers to the Area Managers. Along with trends in center attendance, repayment rates are an early warning signal that center discipline is breaking down and that intervention is needed to bring it back on course.

Conclusion

Grameen Bank, as noted, has a divided vision. It is a bank and it is a poverty alleviation organization. The model it uses predicts that provision of small scale credit can alleviate poverty, and can be delivered in a commercially viable fashion, allowing Branch Banks to achieve profitability. A high level of sound loan disbursements and membership correlate with normal Branch profitability. The ability to sustain high rates of sound loan disbursements and maintain membership is seen as dependent on the quality of the centers and groups, or of center "discipline". Center discipline contributes both to sound financial transactions but also empowers the members to carry out other social, non-financial programs that reduce their poverty and powerlessness.

What does all this mean for a management style that empowers the field staff? The Bank planning and control systems (including its management information system) are designed and operated to give field staff responsibility and the means for building and maintaining center discipline. Empowerment and participation occur within the framework of Bank operations. Field staff, from center members to Area Managers, participate in setting performance goals for the coming year and for the five year plan, but the nature of the goals is pre-determined by the Bank's established operations.

The Bank's formal and informal management information systems collect data on performance indicators ranging from indicators of the quality of center discipline (center attendance, weekly repayment, ability of center members to conduct a meeting); to indicators of branch efficiency (amount of deposit by day in commercial banks, performance against planned budget, number of Bank Assistants per center, manager staff relationships); to indicators of Branch profitability (amount and rate of loan disbursements and repayments, growth in membership). The information, particularly quantitative information on performance indicators, is widely distributed in regular, monthly reports to field managers (Area Managers and Branch Managers) with structured opportunities to discuss the information in monthly meetings. Not only is the information on performance available to the field operators allowing them to identify problems, but the information comes in enough detail for them to discover the nature of the performance problems to be solved. Having the information along with a commit-

161

ment to the goals and direction of the organization, Grameen staff are empowered to focus on discipline and center discipline as the key to quality performance in the Bank.

Notes

1. In general terms one can identify two opposing types of planning and control systems: performance control, which is concerned with monitoring results, and action planning, which specifies the activities that will take place. Action planning is a top-down approach, while performance planning is both bottom-up and top-down. With performance planning, objectives may be set by senior leadership, but units at lower levels set their own targets according to the organizational standard. As individual unit goals are aggregated, there may be an iterative process of negotiation and of adjusting both organizational goals and unit targets. See Henry Mintzberg, **The Structuring of Organizations** (Englewood Cliffs, N.J.: Prentice-Hall, Inc., 1979), 148-149.

2. Aminul Islam, Area Manager, Bhuyapur, Grameen Bank, Interview by author, 29 April 1991.

3. Description of the process is taken from several Grameen Bank documents and forms, including budget and planning forms, guidelines on the Planning System and the Budgeting System; as well as on interviews by the author with Masud Isa, Assistant General Manager, Planning, Dhaka, 2 May 1991.

4. Grameen Bank Phase III Annual Review Mission, **Final Report** and **Working Paper 1, Review of Financial Performance and Projections** (Dhaka: November 1990).

5. Mohammed Mortuza, Deputy General Manager, Monitoring and Evaluation, and Masud Isa, Assistant General Manager, Planning, Grameen Bank, Interviews by author, Dhaka, 17 March, 25 April 1991.

6. Zonal Manager, Bogra, Informal discussions with author, Bogra Zone, 13 December 1990.

7. Shahjahan, Assistant General Manager, Audit Department, Grameen Bank, Interview by author, Dhaka, 18 March 1991.

8. Shahjahan, Interview by author, Dhaka, 18 March 1991.

9. Mozammul Huq, General Manager, Grameen Bank; and Nurjahan, Director, Training Institute, Grameen Bank, Interviews by author,

Dhaka, 19 April 1991 and 17 March 1991.
10. Huq, Interview by author, 19 April 1991.
11. Zubairul Huq, Deputy General Manager, Central Accounts, Grameen Bank, Interview by author, Dhaka, 25 April 1991.
12. Aminul Islam, Interview by author, 30 April 1991.

9

LEARNING FROM GRAMEEN

...the coexistence of firm central control and having individual
autonomy - what we have called "having one's cake and eating it
too."[1]

The lessons of Grameen experience are not so different from the
lessons of exemplary management elsewhere. What is remarkable
about Grameen is that these lessons are demonstrated so successfully
in an organization that works in the villages of one of the poorest
countries of the world.

Extracting Lessons

In reviewing the lessons of Grameen, a series of guiding propositions
emerge. **Grameen Bank is at once highly centralized and highly
decentralized; at once tightly controlled and loosely controlled.**
This dichotomy seems paradoxical, but it is the tight control of the
direction and the values of the organization that allows loose control of
operations.

**Vision and values are important, and managing them is a
primary responsibility of managers.** Knowing where the organization
is going is the essential first step. Grameen managers invest time and
resources in communicating vision. There is remarkable consistency
between the vision articulated by senior management and that espoused
by field managers and staff. Together they express a commitment to
reducing poverty, to changing the lives of the poor, and of increasing
their capacity to control their own destinies. They identify small scale
credit, based on the discipline of small groups, as the mechanism for
alleviating poverty.

Poverty alleviation, as already noted, is not simply raising the
incomes of poor people. Poverty alleviation also means the political
and psychological changes that allow poor people to participate.
Poverty alleviation organizations are in the business of changing values,
of changing culture. To do so, organizations must start first with their

164

own culture. **The values of a poverty alleviation organization must be consistent with its vision.** Poverty alleviation means facilitating the participation and empowerment of the poor. This assumes a belief in the capacities and worth of all people, whatever their status. On a philosophical plane, a belief in the potential of people is indivisible. On a practical plane, valuing the potential contributions of staff, taking them seriously, is expanding the power of the organization to perform at the grassroots.

Grameen leadership is essentially creating and maintaining an organizational culture that differs from that of the surrounding society. Distinctive characteristics of the Grameen culture are a belief in the capacities and worth of all people whatever their status; a commitment to experimentation, learning and innovation; openness and transparency; and a commitment to honesty and to working with the least privileged members of society. This culture provides a framework for autonomy at the field level.

Managing motivation is a priority function of senior managers and field managers. For most poverty alleviation organizations, resources are limited. Money, in the form of bonuses or premiums, cannot be used as a "carrot" to perform rigorous field work. In any case, money is not the primary motivating force. Senior management relies on the experiential, field-based induction training as the starting point for building staff motivation. Induction training is a self-selection process. If, after experiencing the real work of Grameen Bank, recruits decide that they are not prepared to perform the field work, they may select themselves out and resign. For those staff who remain, management sustains motivation for effective and uncorrupted performance under difficult rural conditions using a variety of formal and informal rewards.

In Grameen Bank the sources of motivation are varied. Opportunities for recognition of their work; opportunities for rapid advancement; pride in being part of an organization performing valued work that is recognized internationally; and a sense of belonging to a distinctive group are among the factors contributing to field staff motivation.

Within this framework of shared vision and values, basic operating decisions can be decentralized, and field staff empowered to carry out the basic work of the organization. In Grameen Bank, basic operating decisions on loans and savings are decentralized to the operating level and diffused among staff and clients. The routines and traditions of the organization give boundaries to the core work. Within those core boundaries field staff have considerable autonomy to determine how they will carry out their basic tasks and make the decisions. The diffusion of responsibility to staff and clients can be seen as an actualization of organizational values, of trusting the capacities of operating level staff. The key requirement of staff is meeting organizational goals (see below) and respecting organizational values; the field staff decide how they will meet those goals. Managers in the field push problems down for solution at the functional level.

This is an unusual feature of decentralization at Grameen Bank. Participation in decision-making and other core work is diffused to clients. **Grameen organizational boundaries are permeable; clients are effectively brought into the organization to monitor and be held accountable for loans and other functions.**

Grameen Bank has as its basic operation the delivery of small scale credit and savings services to the poorest rural people in their villages. This poses an apparent paradox; Grameen is a bank but it is also a poverty alleviation organization. It is delivering services to the poorest, but it has as an objective commercial viability. The two may not always be consistent. Grameen Bank resolves this apparent paradox through the **clarity on its core task**. Understanding why this dual vision is not a paradox, and how that apparent paradox is resolved in the simple, operating task of the organization, helps to explain what is distinctive about Grameen Bank and clarifies the nature of participation and empowerment in Grameen Bank.

The field managers of Grameen explain the paradox most clearly. When asked what performance indicators they use to monitor Branch Bank functioning, Area Managers and Branch Managers uniformly responded, "discipline". Discipline means regular attendance at center meetings, which leads to regular repayment of loans. Regular repayment assumes that the borrower was able to earn enough from her investment to repay the loan. Repayment maintains the cash flow and the viability of Bank operations. It also means that borrowers are becoming disciplined, responsible and increasingly autonomous. Out of the discipline they gain a financial and psychological control over their own lives. Grameen staff share in the discipline and the accountability by ensuring the discipline of the groups, centers and Branches. **Being held accountable, for loan repayment or for center performance, is "being taken seriously".** If you are taken seriously, you gain in status.

Grameen Bank operations are marked by transparency and

openness. This transparency is most visible in the way in which banking operations are conducted in the open in front of groups of borrowers and/or bank staff. The formal and informal information systems operating in Grameen enable openness, and also serve as the information circulatory system that allow this centralized - decentralized configuration to work productively. The formal information system, described in Chapter 8, performs two key functions. It generates information that allows senior management to monitor whether the decentralized operating units are together achieving organization goals. The system also feeds information back to the operators so that they can regulate performance in relation to their own goals, and to what they see their peers accomplishing. The informal information system also operates in both directions. Through organizational myths and stories and through hearsay, organizational values are communicated to field staff. More importantly, the informal system generates a flow of qualitative information about performance and practice up the hierarchy. Informal communication takes many forms, from letters to casual chatter between senior managers visiting the field and lower level staff. It serves to validate information from other sources, and it validates Grameen's espoused focus on the operating staff. Someone is listening to the informal information that bubbles up.

Managers of poverty alleviation work must model participatory and empowering management. Organizational traditions at Grameen encourage managers to adopt empowering behaviors. Chapter 5 suggested that national and bureaucratic cultures in Bangladesh are centralizing, hierarchical, fatalistic and biased against women. Participatory approaches are a break with these traditional practices in the country. Chapters 4 and 6 described the formal and informal rituals and procedures in Grameen that help break down tradition and to facilitate participation. Senior managers model good listening and non-hierarchical behaviors; their models are adopted by some, though not all, field managers. Traditional Grameen practices, if not always written as rules, establish patterns of rotating center leadership, individual member responsibility for knowledge of bank rules and of the Sixteen Decisions. Field managers cannot meet the requirements of work without regular interaction with centers, Bank workers and other staff. The common decision-making process on loan approvals requires the participation of all relevant individuals, from client to Area Manager, in the decision process. Informal practices legitimize communication across hierarchical lines and provide practical ways for

SIX COMMANDMENTS
FOR MANAGING
POVERTY ALLEVIATION

1. The leadership of poverty alleviation organizations should exercise tight, central control over the vision and values of the organization.

2. Control over and accountability for basic operations should be devolved to the operating level. Participation will be diffused across organizational boundaries and include clients as well as staff.

*3. Poverty alleviation organizations must believe in the capacities of people to achieve results **and** to be held accountable. Organizations must practice, and be seen to practice, the values that they espouse.*

4. The basic work of the organization should be simple and clear. Staff at all levels need simple indicators and adequate information to evaluate performance against objectives.

5. Operations must be open and transparent.

6. Managers need a methodology and an explicit strategy for enabling participatory and empowering management behaviors.

junior staff to raise controversial issues with senior staff. The induction training requires recruits to experience directly the values of the organization. They are immediately thrown into field work, living close to their clients. They learn about poverty and Grameen's operations by asking questions, listening and observing. They do not learn by lectures. They are required to take responsibility for teaching themselves.

Putting participation and empowerment in management into practice requires a methodology. There may be explicit or implicit resistance to participation from the managers, or even from staff. Participation occurs when organization leaders think about daily actions that encourage or program managers to listen, to include women staff, or to welcome new ideas from others. It occurs when field managers consciously create the opportunities for field staff to contribute, and when field managers demonstrate that they value field staff by holding them responsible for performance.

Senior management in poverty alleviation organizations must manage the environment in which the organization works. It must also be future oriented. It must take the strategic actions today that assure the capacity of the organization in the future. While senior managers and field managers were found to articulate the same vision of Grameen Bank as a poverty alleviation organization, there was a difference. Senior managers were actively involved in shaping the future vision of the Bank, and in insulating the core work from disruptions outside the organization.

The breadth of the organizational vision was always expanding to respond to its changing situation. Once the core technology of credit and savings operations were established in the first decade of operations, senior management began to think about second generation borrowing, larger scale enterprises and higher technologies. More recently, senior managers have come to stress efforts to influence national policies so that they benefit or at least impact equitably on the poor. They see the need for expanding agricultural productivity and overall economic growth.

At the same time senior management has worked to protect Grameen work in the villages from external threats. This has meant specific responses such as managing a response to an attempt to unionize field staff which would have required rigid working hours that are ill-suited to serving poor, village clients. They built an international recognition of the work of Grameen. That recognition assures international support and funding as well as shields the Bank from outside interference.

Applying Lessons

The lessons of Grameen are already being applied.[2] As a specific model, Grameen is being applied in the developing world, and in North America and Europe. This study cannot assess those replications. What is significant is that groups committed to poverty alleviation have taken the Grameen working model and adapted it to their own circumstances. Their experience will demonstrate the validity of the Grameen model of targeted credit and its transferability.

This book puts forward some propositions about how the Grameen model is managed. Beyond that, it argues that the management approaches of Grameen Bank are transferable across cultures. More than that, the experience of Grameen management offers broader lessons to developed as well as developing countries about how we can structure our organizations to serve the public; and about how we can put into practice some of the values commonly espoused.

Most development professionals have observed the interaction of national culture with the operation of bureaucratic structures. The question has often been raised about the transferability of Western management principles to non-Western settings. The experience of Grameen, in a non-Western setting and with a strong traditional culture, suggests that we may be asking the question the wrong way. It may be more useful to adopt a positive perspective. What are the principles of human management which we see applied across cultures? What are the adjustments we see in the application of these principles, and under what circumstances? A remarkable aspect of Grameen management practices is their resemblance to the prescriptions of current practitioner and strategic quality management literature.

Valuing the capacities of people - whether staff or clients - was seen to be a dominant value of Grameen Bank practice. Talking about such organizational values in the poverty alleviation context risks criticisms of being inconsequential. Values are difficult to define and measure. Valuing individuals for their potential capacity to contribute to organization goals can be seen as empowering of staff.

Valuing operational level staff has become important in the private sector for practical reasons. Peters, Drucker and others suggest that in an economic and technological environment characterized by constant change, an organization needs the flexibility at the operating level to adjust rapidly to emerging opportunities and constraints. One corporate executive referred to the current environment as one "...where we must have every good idea from every man and women in the organization, we cannot afford management styles that suppress and intimidate".[3]

Quality management writers assert that quality is everyone's business and that quality is best achieved by engaging the participation of operating level staff and managers. Juran, for example, pointed out that responsibility for quality needs to be delegated to individuals who take ownership of the quality. The conditions for doing so are knowing what the goals are, having the information to know what performance against goals is, and having the capacity to influence performance when it falls short of goals.[4] Implicit in delegating is the reciprocal function of holding staff accountable.

Valuing the capacity of field staff to achieve organization goals serves organization purposes. It can also meet the needs of staff to be part of a productive enterprise that serves valued goals larger than themselves. In this sense, Grameen demonstrates the counter-intuitive link between discipline and accountability on the one hand, and participation and empowerment on the other. Participation and empowerment imply autonomy and control for the individual. Discipline suggests adherence to (someone else's) requirements. The Grameen experience demonstrates, as Peters suggested elsewhere, that "autonomy is a product of discipline".

Discipline that Grameen staff talk about is not an imposed discipline, but a shared discipline. The discipline for Grameen members is regular center attendance and regular repayment. It is responsibility for one's loan and for the loans of the group and the center. It is the Bank Worker's responsibility for his/her centers. Implicit in this concept of discipline is that discipline, and the autonomy it allows, will produce a quality product, or meaning, from which the worker can derive satisfaction. This is what appears to happen for many of the field managers and staff in Grameen Bank.

Impetus for participatory and empowering management may come from the negative experience of bureaucracies that are rule-bound, hierarchical and disempowering. The search for participatory and empowering alternatives is not an effort to discard rules. Rules can have empowering potential. The Grameen experience suggests that when vision, values and an understanding of rules and procedures are

171

shared, rules can facilitate work rather than work serving rules. In this circumstance rules can create a discipline that is empowering. This is an approach that perhaps explains the enthusiasm Grameen has generated among supporters who hold a range of political outlooks.

Finally, a larger lesson of Grameen is that the time for creating new paradigms is not over. Grameen has created a new paradigm of banking services. It is a paradigm that works because it values and empowers those who implement it, and because its values permeate implementation. Grameen has, as founder Yunus promised, turned banking upside down. What makes this model of banking revolutionary is that it takes banking services to the clients in the village, rather than asking them to come to the bank. It adapts the regulations to the potentials of clients rather than asking clients to adapt to rules intended for male, literate elites. Most importantly, its banking efforts are concentrated on the period after the loan rather than before. It is more concerned with supporting the client through the repayment period than with detailed and lengthy appraisal of loan proposals. This means building a system that supports the successful implementation of small enterprises funded by loans. It means systems that encourage discipline and regularity.

As global societies, North and South, we must examine our institutions. We need to ask what purposes they serve. And we need to have the imagination to turn them upside down so that we can contribute to building a sustainable future. This is the lesson of Grameen.

Notes

1. Thomas J. Peters and Robert H. Waterman Jr., **In Search of Excellence: Lessons from America's Best-run Companies** (New York: Harper and Row, 1982), 318.
2. For example, see I.P. Getubig, M. Yaakub Johari, Angela M. Kuga Thas, **Overcoming Poverty Through Credit, The Asian Experience in Replicating the Grameen Bank Approach** (Kuala Lumpur: Asian and Pacific Development Centre, 1993).
3. John Holusha, "A Softer 'Neutron Jack' at G.E.", New York **Times,** 4 March 1992, p.D1.
4. J.M. Juran, **Juran on Leadership for Quality: An Executive Handbook,** (New York: The Free Press, a Division of Macmillan, Inc., 1989), 147-148.

APPENDIX

ORGANIZATIONAL RESEARCH
AT THE GRASSROOTS

No matter how much research money you have, or how many assistants you
may hire, always handle your own rat.

Organizations and their behavior are complex. Large, grassroots
sector corporations. Their technology may be simple and their annual
budgets smaller, but poverty alleviation organizations face the same generic management problems, though with fewer resources, as the
private sector.

Robert Yin argues that the case study method may be the most
effective method to study complex organizational phenomena. Despite
a stereotype of case studies as a weak sister to other methodologies,
Yin argues they can be rigorous, objective and precise while having
advantages in getting at the "how" and the "why" questions of
research.

Mintzberg, as noted before, argues for the benefits of studying the
complex reality of organizations on a case by case basis rather than in
large sample, with "gross, cross-sectional measures". He urges the
development of theory "that grows inductively out of systematic in-
vestigation of how organizations behave". He asserts that

...we shall never understand the complex reality of organizations
if we persist in studying them from a distance, in large samples
with gross, cross-sectional measures. We learn how birds fly
by studying them one at a time, not by scanning flocks of them
on radar screens.

Bailey noted that "the laboratories of public administration are the
offices of practitioners" and argued for a practitioner-oriented research
with critical analysis and rigorous methodology. To borrow Grice's
metaphor, if you are going to study managers, you had better observe
them in action.

This research was sparked by a seemingly simple question: do

173

organizations dedicated to the empowerment and participation of the poor in developing countries themselves have an empowering and participatory management? The question seems simple, but it is not. First empowerment and participation carry many and sometimes conflicting interpretations. Researching empowerment and participation is a bit like playing with child's clay. Perfectly malleable, the definitions seem to be able to adapt their shape to the purposes at hand. What do participation and empowerment mean if their definition is dependent on the situation?

Secondly, the organization and management literature is unclear as to whether participatory and empowering management contributes to the efficiency and/or effectiveness of reaching organization goals. The Human Relations school of thought certainly believes that participation and empowerment are desirable human ideals. The quality management literature and case studies put the participation of the operating staff at the heart of achieving quality. But research on industrial democracy, for example, does not make a clear case for inherent efficiency of participatory management. Partly the problem is one of definition. It also is a reflection of value systems.

Participation and empowerment remain the politically correct attributes of poverty alleviation work, whether we know or agree on their meaning, and whether we believe they contribute to effectiveness and efficiency. Because they are widely held values or aspirations they cry out for systematic description of how they operate in a specific organizational situation. This research selects one of the growing number of indigenous poverty alleviation organizations that have emerged in increasing numbers in the Third World during the past two decades to address the problems of persistent poverty. It seeks to look systematically at the "how" of organizing and managing poverty alleviation, and the nature of participation and empowerment in managing the implementation of poverty alleviation in one organization.

Identifying an Organization

To explore participatory and empowering management in one organization committed to poverty alleviation required identifying a suitable subject for study. Selection criteria included organizational commitment to poverty alleviation that encompassed participation and empowerment of the poor; evidence that the interventions of the organization had resulted in poverty alleviation, including participation and empowerment, for its intended clients; and a size and scope of work that would make findings at least relevant but perhaps generalizable to a discussion of medium to large scale poverty alleviation interventions. There were also practical considerations of language and accessibility.

Grameen Bank in Bangladesh met the criteria (see Chapter 3 for discussion of the Bank) and agreed to accommodate the proposed research. Grameen is a poverty alleviation organization, registered as a Bank, that in 1991 was making small loans to nearly one million very poor rural people. Its outreach surpasses that of many government departments in Bangladesh and elsewhere. There is empirical evidence of Grameen Bank impact on the income and assets of its clients, as well as on their participation and empowerment. The international development community recognizes its record of extending loans, of achieving repayment rates in excess of 98 percent, of generating savings, of building group cohesion, and of enabling access or entitlement to resources for growing numbers of poor Bangladeshis.

Grameen also illustrates some of the paradoxes of participation and empowerment noted in Chapter 2. Supporters of Grameen Bank praise it for participatory management and operations that empower staff. Detractors argue that it is hierarchical, dependent on the leadership of its founder-Managing Director, and that its work is highly regimented, not participatory and empowering. Grameen itself embodies the question of what participation and empowerment mean.

Within Grameen Bank, the research and analysis focus primarily on two levels of managers. The first is the senior management which includes the Head Office Managing Director, Deputy Managing Director, General Manager, Deputy and Assistant General managers and the 9 (in 1991) Zonal Managers. Subject to the broad policy direction of the Grameen Bank Board, this level defines policy approaches and operational strategies. The second level is that of Area Managers, a geographically dispersed level of middle managers. Area Managers report to Zonal Managers and are themselves responsible for about ten Branch Banks. The Area Managers have a direct management role, not only with subordinate staff, but also with clients. Area Managers interact with clients at specific occasions (group recognition, loan utilization inspection). Their management behaviors need to be seen not only in relation to staff but also to clients and their role with clients as a likely behavior model for subordinates.

Appendix

There are practical and strategic reasons for focusing on these two levels of the organization. Language was a key factor limiting access. Without a working knowledge of Bangla, the national language in Bangladesh, the researcher was practically limited to working with Grameen Bank staff who can function in English. There are 2,323 officers or manager level staff in Grameen Bank (December 1990). Nearly all of these have a master's degree that was done in English. Initially it was intended to focus on the lowest level of managers, the Branch Managers, who supervise six to ten or more staff working from the Bank Branch. Preliminary interviews and a trial observation of a Branch Manager and an Area manager in the first field visit suggested the possibility that the presence of an observer interfered substantially with the work and responses of the Branch Manager. Branch Managers may have only short tenure and be serving in their first posting. Area Managers are likely to have had at least two previous postings with Grameen and to have worked on previous occasions with foreign visitors. Area Managers met during the initial visit were clearly more comfortable in dealing with foreign observers.

Strategically there are advantages to studying the Area Managers. Area Managers, it can be argued, function as operating core managers, coordinating the work of the normally ten branch banks or core units within an Area. They exercise final clearance on routine operating decisions; they monitor performance; and they play key motivating and problem solving functions.

An essentially inductive approach has been used to study participation and empowerment in the management of poverty alleviation intervention. Inductive case study approaches are thought to be useful for studying organizational dynamics within single settings. The implications of this approach are an openness to new concepts and relationships while maintaining a systematic approach so as to avoid being overwhelmed by data. Kathleen M. Eisenstadt suggests that "theory building research is begun as close as possible to the ideal of no theory under consideration and no hypotheses to test". She recognizes the difficulty of that ideal and suggests that the researcher begin with a research problem and pose some potentially important variables, with reference to the relevant literature. At the outset, researchers should avoid making relationships among the variables. Daft urges the student of organizations to be open to "surprises". He points to reviews of landmark studies in the behavioral and organizational sciences that suggest that they tended to be "loosely done". "The significant studies often approached the problem as an open-ended question to be answered rather than as an hypothesis to be tested".

Open-ended should not be equated with unsystematic and not rigorous. Daft calls this type of research a craft, with elements of openness to surprise, storytelling, non-linear decision-making, common sense, and "research poetry" that provide a framework. Schein talks about an "iterative" research process in uncovering the cultural assumptions that underlie behavior in an organization. Participation and empowerment can be seen as a special case of cultural assumptions supporting behavior in an organization. Schein argues that exploring the cultural assumptions must be a joint enterprise of an insider and an outsider to the organization culture, each enabling the other to uncover blind spots and, step by step, to reach better understanding of reality. Schein says that there is no "reliable, quick way" to uncover cultural assumptions. Instead he suggests an iterative interviewing process, supported by other sources of information.

As will become evident below, this research has followed an iterative approach to a case study that began with an open-ended question.

An Iterative Process in Action

To understand the iterative model of inquiry used in this study, it is more useful to think of a spiral rather than of a line. While the logic of linear thinking is powerfully attractive, it may not be the way in which we humans actually learn. Jerome Bruner, who has spent his professional life studying how people learn, suggested we learn in a spiral, going over the same material but at ever increasing levels of complexity.

This research began with questions about the meaning of empowerment and participation in managing poverty alleviation. It was spurred on by the general question of whether poverty alleviation organizations which seek the participation and empowerment of the poor must themselves be participatory and empowering in their management. At the outset it was informed by the management literature which suggested that several variables from the management literature might serve as indicators of the extent and nature of participation and empowerment in the management of poverty alleviation organizations. These variables are the vision or goals of the organization, its values, motivation, and aspects of the structuring, decision-making, job design and planning and control systems. These variables, along with preliminary research and a chance to interview the Managing Director of Grameen Bank in Washington, determined the preliminary research questions:

- What are the vision and values of Grameen Bank? How and by whom are they articulated? To what extent do the staff share, both in expression and in their work, the vision and values of the leadership?
- Is Grameen Bank truly able to retain staff working under difficult circumstances with poor clients in rural areas? Is the organization free of corruption, in contrast to the surrounding environment? What motivates staff to willingness to undertake daily work in the villages and to integrity in an environment where pressures to do otherwise are strong?
- Who holds decision-making power? Where are decisions on basic work made? Are they made at the operating level, or are they referred up the hierarchy?
- How much latitude for creativity, innovation, or response to opportunities is there at the operating level? Are operating staff able to learn from experience and adjust their work procedures, or is all work specified in detail by the organization?

These general questions were the starting point for the preliminary field work, scheduled for the first three weeks of December 1990. Street demonstrations in Dhaka which led to the resignation of President Ershad in the first week of December, curtailed the number of interviews. They did not, in fact, alter the overall plan for the preliminary research. This included review of documentation on Grameen Bank, including the reports prepared for a just completed donor review mission; interviews with the Managing Director and General Manager and a limited number of Head Office staff; a day visit to one Branch Bank; and a week long visit to one Area where there were opportunities to test research methodologies with an Area Manager and a Branch Manager, as well as to attend a one day training session for Bank Workers.

The field research tools to be tested included a structured interview guide for managers at different levels; a preliminary guide for recording observations of field managers; two draft questionnaires on manager attitudes and practices tentatively designed for Area or Branch Managers; and a standard questionnaire, based on the Blake Mouton Grid, for discovering management style. At this point the research tools were related only in a general way to the research questions. In particular, it was expected that the structured interviews would initially produce a broad picture of how Grameen Bank operates. The questions were loosely based on Mintzberg's concept of organizational framework, which it was expected would guide analysis of how the organization works. The structured observations were expected to provide the most useful and original information about what managers really do in Grameen Bank. The techniques were tested with one Branch Manager and one Area Manager to determine whether it could be done by an outsider speaking only English; what kinds of data could be gathered by a non-Bangla speaker; what preliminary forms of structure might be imposed on the observations; and whether in general the observations would produce useful information.

The survey questionnaire and the management style questionnaire were also tested, but only in part, with several managers. On the last day of the visit, the researcher had the opportunity to present initial findings and to discuss the research plan for the second visit in a meeting that included the Managing Director and all senior managers who were in Dhaka at the time. This was an opportunity not only to check on conclusions, but also to obtain their support for the second stage.

The experience of the preliminary research produced findings about research methodology which guided planning for the second visit and which remained valid during the second visit. The first finding was that Grameen Staff at all levels were open to interviews and prepared to invest considerable amounts of time in answering any questions asked. In part this reflects the verbal nature of Bangladeshi (Bengali) culture. It also represented, for most, an enthusiasm about Grameen work and a real interest in explaining it to a foreigner. The fact that Grameen was being researched was a validation of the worth of their work. This affected the nature of structured interviews. A single question would spark a long answer that touched on many issues. In the end the interview guide was not a questionnaire but a tally sheet as to whether important issues were covered.

The structured observation technique was based on a methodology developed by Mintzberg in his 1969 study of five CEOs in North America.[8] Testing the method identified problems and led to adaptations. Verbosity and the presence of a foreigner had a negative impact on the structured observation technique. During testing in the preliminary field research, the Branch Manager was uneasy with having me sit quietly taking notes, and felt obliged to interrupt with long explanations of what he was doing. The Area Manager was less disturbed by the presence of an outsider. He was able to carry out his normal work without significant distraction.

Language was also a problem. If a question was asked about the nature of a conversation (in Bangla) or the content of a piece of correspondence, the natural flow of work was interrupted. In this sense it was not possible to follow Mintzberg's model of accounting for the exact amount of time devoted to each piece of paper, conversation, task or problem. It was found possible to measure fairly accurately the time devoted to specific categories of tasks, such as paperwork, Center meetings, informal discussions with Center members or with Bank Workers, supervision of loan utilization, or travelling. It was possible at odd moments and at the end of the day to review any questions about the general nature of activities taking place.

Initially it was planned to conduct a survey of field managers to collect data from a representative group on their attitudes and practices. Additionally it was planned to administer a management style questionnaire to a selected sample of Area Managers to develop evidence on managers' descriptions of their own management styles. The preliminary field work demonstrated that these survey tools are ill-suited to the Bangladesh and Grameen Bank environment. It was possible to test only a part of each instrument with a few Managers in December. Each question aroused questions and spirited discussion which precluded completing the questionnaire. In all cases there were problems with the language and with question and answer construction. While the managers could all work in English, it was not clear that the concepts used in the questions meant the same thing to them as they did to an outsider, or even to a fellow manager. Many managers were not comfortable with scalar answers. They tended to give answers at the extreme of the scale when experience or earlier conversation with them suggested that their answers would be somewhere in the middle. Questions which asked managers to evaluate their superiors made some managers uncomfortable.

The testing experience and the final review meeting with Grameen senior management in December suggested dropping the questionnaires. The questionnaires were dropped, but some of the questions were used during informal interviews to spark discussions. Additionally, the experience of spending a week living, eating, working and resting in a Grameen Bank Area revealed that there would be many unplanned opportunities for observing Bank Managers, interviewing Bank Workers at all levels, and for establishing a relationship with Bank staff. Sharing meals, playing badminton, sleeping in the same facility, bouncing over dirt roads on the back of a motorcycle or bicycle, joining an Area Manager on a visit to his wife, also a Grameen Bank Officer posted in a different location, all create human dynamics very different from those that Mintzberg must have confronted while observing his five CEOs in their offices. The circumstances more nearly approach those of the anthropologist, and allow the outsider to enter into the life of the Bank manager. They also dramatize the degree to which Grameen Bank employment dominates the existence of managers, obliterating for many the boundaries between personal and professional life. This has an impact on how data collected should be analyzed.

The first research visit influenced the second by establishing the principal research tools ultimately used. First it led to a focus of the interview guide on questions exploring the reward systems at Grameen, performance planning systems and performance measures used; the information system and how and by whom it is used, and decision-making systems. Secondly it affirmed a decision to employ a research assistant to assist with and duplicate the structured observations. The assistant, to be recruited from the Institute of Business Administration at the University of Dhaka, would bring language and cultural fluency along with an understanding of basic management issues to an exploration of what Area Managers actually do. His or her structured observations could also serve as a check on the validity of those performed by an outside observer. Third, the initial visit led to an alternative to the survey and management skill questionnaires that would allow data collection from a large number of Area Managers. Out of the final review meeting in December 1990 came the suggestion from Grameen senior management to hold what were essentially focus group discussions with Area Managers in four Areas (Bogra, Rangpur, Dinajpur and Dhaka). Finally, the research continued to seek out documents or artifacts relevant to the variables.

As the research progressed there was an attempt to use multiple research methodologies to explore any one variable. These methodologies are summarized in Table A.

Table A. Research Methodologies by Variables Studied

	Structured Observation	Interviews			Focus Groups	Documents
		Sr. Mgrs.	Area Mgrs.	Others		
Articulated vision		x	x	x	x	x
Vision in practice	x		x	x		
Articulated values		x	x	x	x	
Values in practice	x		x	x		
Motivation	x	x	x	x	x	x
Decision making	x	x	x	x	x	x
Planning/Performance	x	x	x	x	x	x

While the research process was iterative in terms of refining questions and concepts, the basic methodology of structured interviews, observation, focus group discussions and analysis of documentation remained the same throughout the second field visit (March 15 to May 3, 1991).

The framework for the initial interviews in Grameen Head Office was the starting point and it remained the overall framework. As answers to some of the questions emerged, the questions themselves were tightened and deepened. From general questions on problem solving, the questioning moved to specific problems: how do you solve a problem of non-payment of a loan? Questions on reward systems and performance indicators moved to identification of particular Grameen Bank information systems and documents, or they identified specific data, as on promotion rates, which Grameen Bank staff especially retrieved for this study. Questions that were originally intended for a limited set of staff, such as those on orientation and training, were asked of a large variety of staff to validate perceptions. Interviews with Head Office staff were conducted before, in the middle of and after all field research. There was an opportunity for a final, one hour meeting with the Managing Director of Grameen Bank to present preliminary conclusions and test their validity against his perceptions.

The field experience gave countless, unexpected opportunities for informal interviews and observations. Branch Managers came to the Area Manager's home for afternoon or evening discussions and stayed to talk about their own work. Auditors were auditing a Branch visited and interrupted to talk about their work in general. A union organizer sought out the researcher to explain the union position on organizing the non-officers in Grameen Bank. These encounters all added to the perspective of the study and often offered an additional opportunity to test findings.

Head Office interviews were, with one or two exceptions, tape recorded. Shortly after the interviews, summary notes were made from the tapes and typed up. Outside of Dhaka, notes on formal and informal interviews were kept in chronological notebooks or diaries and were transcribed at the earliest possible moment or within one month of return from the field.

A tentative schedule had been worked out with Grameen Bank for three five to six day observations each of Area Managers by the researcher and assistant as well as focus group discussions at four Zonal meetings.

Appendix

The five Areas chosen for observation were in three different Zones. The Zones were selected because they represented three different stages in Grameen Bank development. Tangail is the oldest Zone in Grameen Bank and has well established management patterns and traditions. It has the highest number of profitable Branches. Dinajpur is a new zone experiencing growth and with new branches opening. Bogra Zone has been operational for several years and has Branches moving toward the stage when they should be profitable. Logistically, the three Zones made sense. It was possible to conduct observations on two managers in Bogra during the last week in March and attend the monthly Zonal Meetings of Area Managers in Bogra, Rangpur and Dinajpur, scheduled sequentially to accommodate this research, during the first week of April.

The second set of observations was conducted the second week of April in Dinajpur. It lost a day at the beginning because of a public holiday, and was concluded a day early because of the holiday marking the end of Ramadan. There was a ten day break in field work because of the Eid holiday. This was used to interview additional Head Office Staff, and re-interview others.

The third set of observations was conducted in Tangail Zone in the last week of April. A holiday abbreviated this set of observations to four days. The final focus group discussion was held in Dhaka Zone during the May Zonal meeting.

Additionally four days were spent carrying out a structured observation with a Save the Children (USA) field manager, working at an equivalent level to Grameen Bank Area managers. The object was to develop similar data on field managers in another poverty alleviation organization in Bangladesh.

Designing and implementing the structured observations was the most difficult task for two reasons. First it involved transposing Mintzberg's technique from a fairly standard North American corporate setting across language and culture to operational level management in an unconventional poverty alleviation bank. Second, it required orienting a Bangladeshi research assistant in a short time to a novel research technique. Initially expectations were greater than what reality permitted. It had been hoped to be able to categorize by very precise time periods the exact role the Area Managers were playing, using Mintzberg's classification of managerial roles for coding. When the first observation began in the second research visit, the procedures for the structured interviews were very simple:

1. Explain to the Area Manager being observed the purpose of the observation - "to find out what Area Managers really do"; and stress that the success of the research depended on the Area managers strictly following their normal routine.
2. Take careful notes on each general category of activity by amount of time involved; persons involved; location; actions being performed; and the function of the manager being observed. (All categories of activity could not be specified ahead of time, but they were expected to include travel, desk work [by type where possible without interrupting the flow of work], branch visits, formal and informal discussions with Bank staff, Center meetings, Group recognition meetings and loan utilization inspections.)
3. To the extent possible during each activity note whether the Manager was supportive or directive. Supporting is evidenced by praise, recognition, listening or assisting subordinates to solve problems or strengthen work. Directive was defined as giving orders or telling.
4. Finally, and to the extent possible, take notes on anything else observed that seemed relevant.

Selecting, orienting and supervising the assistant researcher was essential to the validity of the findings. Selection was done totally on the recommendation of a professor at the Institute for Business Administration, Dhaka, who was both familiar with Grameen Bank and with North American management literature through his own study at the Wharton School. Orientation was two-fold. It included a discussion of the research project and aims with the assistant and another management professor who had worked inside a sister poverty alleviation organization in Bangladesh (Bangladesh Rural Advancement Committee), plus an opportunity for the assistant to read Mintzberg's **The Nature of Managerial Work** and particularly Appendix C on methodology. It also included a week-long opportunity to work together with the assistant on putting the structured observation guidelines into operation. The first set of observations were scheduled for Sherpur Area in Bogra District where both researchers stayed at the Area Office, which was also the home of the Area Manager. The assistant was to observe the Program Officer at the same time as the researcher observed the Area Manager. The first day of observation, by earlier design, had the Area Manager and Program Officer travelling together. This allowed note taking on the same events, and a comparison of notes during and after the observation.

During the subsequent five days, the Area Manager and Program Officer, for the most part, followed separate schedules. Each evening, the assistant and the researcher reviewed the field notes on observations and worked to clarify notes and to develop a common approach. The second and third set of observations were conducted in separate locations. Review of the field notes took place immediately following completion of each of these observations.

Focus group discussions were structured by a set of seven questions asked at all four meetings. The order of the questions was altered in attempts to find the question which would most rapidly engage the Area Managers. The Zonal Meetings included not only the Area Managers, but also the Program Officers who report to the Area Managers, and officers of principal officer rank or above posted to the Zonal Office. Although only the participation of Area Managers was originally planned for the focus group discussions, all officers in the room were invited to join in the discussion. The fact that few besides the Area officers did participate becomes a piece of evidence. Questions were asked in both English and Bangla and participants were invited to respond in the language they preferred. Most responded in Bangla. The discussions, ranging in length from one to two hours, were all tape-recorded. As soon as possible, in all but one case immediately, the tapes were replayed, the assistant translated them, and I took detailed notes on his translation. At the end of the focus group discussions the Area Managers, and in one case the Program Officers, completed a brief questionnaire on their length of service, education and socio-economic background. They were also asked whether they discussed the Annual Confidential Review with the subordinates whose performance they were monitoring.

Operationalizing Research

At the outset the research was instigated by general questions on the existence and nature of participatory and empowering management in poverty alleviation work. Supported by a general knowledge of the literature and the practice of poverty alleviation organizations in the Third World, it identified the variables of vision or mission, values, motivation, and the structuring of work as potentially important to describing and explaining the nature of empowering and participatory management. These variables, in general, were operationalized by drawing on both the management and the development literature.

Operationalizing the articulation of vision was straightforward. In an open-ended way, senior managers and Area Managers were asked to define the vision or goals of Grameen Bank. If necessary, managers were asked to specify the income/asset and the empowerment/participation goals for clients. Senior managers were questioned in a series of interviews. Their responses were coded and compared with statements of vision or goals in documents and speeches. Area Managers were approached in a slightly different way. During focus group discussions they were asked, in light of the many functions performed by the Bank, to identify the most important work of Grameen Bank. The focus group discussions were supported by individual interviews with Area Managers. Data from both interview sources and from the analysis of documentation were coded by category of vision (income/asset changes, empowerment, participation) and then analyzed. During the coding there were statements of vision that did not fit into the expected categories. These included senior management strategic vision of the future of the organization. Additionally, sub-categories were created for the different types of empowering and participatory vision held.

Operationalizing vision in action required choices of indicators. If the expressed vision of poverty alleviation is defined as a combination of income changes and empowerment of the poor, then the question becomes one of whether the organization by its actions encourages a balanced effort toward those dual goals of poverty alleviation. Four types of indicators were chosen: articulated performance indicators, formal rewards and two types of informal rewards. In each case the question was about the balance between the banking and the empowerment/participation goals of the Bank. How are articulated performance indicators balanced between banking and empowerment/participation functions? Within the formal reward system, how does the Annual Confidential Review rank performance against financial and empowerment functions? Within the informal reward system, what is the balance between reward or recognition given to financial versus empowerment and participation accomplishments?

Two forms of evidence of informal rewards or recognition were chosen as a result of preliminary research. The first was found in the 'myths' or stories in the Grameen about who and what kind of performance gets recognized. The second was an analysis of what is recognized in **Uddog**, the in-house magazine. Articles in **Uddog** are written by staff at all levels. Initial interviews and observations of staff reading it, suggested that publication in **Uddog** was an opportunity for recognition. Ideally the analysis would have covered issues over an extended period. Language disability and lack of capacity to translate the issues led to a less reliable process. To determine how much emphasis articles gave to banking issues as opposed to empowerment/participation questions, one issue was reviewed in depth with translation assistance. Other issues were briefly reviewed. Area Managers were asked about **Uddog** and the significance of articles in it.

Determining articulated values about ideal management behavior was simple and direct. It involved asking Senior Management and Area Managers about the way in which poverty alleviation should be managed and reading what is said in Bank documents. The Managing Director and founder has spoken at length and written about the values that underlay the foundation of the organization and that he continues to see as essential. Other senior managers were questioned about organization values and ideal management practices. In focus group discussions Area Managers were asked several questions that it was hoped would lead them to verbalize their management values.

The notes on interviews and focus group discussions were analyzed first by breaking out responses that dealt with management values. These were then coded by expected categories of experimentation or learning process approach; listening versus talking; supportive versus directive; enabling; hierarchical versus non-hierarchical behavior. Analysis of what managers said revealed other priorities. Senior managers gave priority to valuing people, whether clients or subordinates. Field managers particularly talked about discipline.

Operationalizing values in action started with three sets of values that emerged from the analysis of articulated values. These are experimentation or a learning process approach; deferring to the operating level personnel; and discipline. The first has its roots in the development management literature; the second is adapted from Tom Peters. The third is a value identified by the Grameen Managers and which has no precise description in the management literature.

To establish whether managers had an experimental or learning approach and what kind of a learning process took place, the notes on observation were analyzed for instances of non-standard situations confronted by the managers and their responses; and examples of managers learning from experience and/or acknowledging problems.

Operationalizing the value of "deferring to the front line", the research used the indicators of listening behaviors, supporting behaviors and non-hierarchical practices. Delegation, or decentralized decision-making, is clearly an aspect of deferring to the front line. This is dealt with in Chapter 7. The field notes on observation were coded to indicate instances of listening, talking, questioning, and inclusiveness as indicators of listening behaviors. For supportive behavior the notes were coded for instances of supporting, recognizing, helping and blaming. Hierarchical behavior was identified by coding for seating position, handshaking and gestures, personal service and other. Matrices were developed to analyze the field notes. Additionally the percentage of time managers spent with subordinates or clients was used as an indicator of deferring to the front line.

Discipline emerged as a value of the Bank and as an indicator during the research. It was a term with specific meaning in the Grameen context and used over and over again by managers to describe their behavior and to describe how they evaluated the performance of subordinates, and of Centers and Groups. Field notes on operations as well as the notes on focus group discussions were analyzed for definitions of discipline, and of how managers used discipline as an indicator of performance.

Motivation is directly linked to vision and values. It explains why staff will adopt and put into action the vision and values of the organization that employs them. This research looked at motivation from three perspectives. First it needed to establish as a reasonable assumption that Grameen Bank successfully motivates its staff to put vision and values into action. The measures of this success include its impact on the target population in terms of income/asset and participation and empowerment objectives. Establishing this assumption relied on a review of the principal evaluations of Grameen Bank. It also included using Grameen Bank and other data to establish that there is low staff turnover (after the initial period) and that there is a low level of corruption.

Secondly, the research explored the principal tools management uses to inculcate and maintain motivation. The tools were identified through asking both senior managers and field managers and staff in formal and informal interviews how management kept staff motivated and how important were different tools of motivation. As the research progressed, it was possible to ask increasingly specific questions about the importance of induction training, and formal and informal reward systems.

This led to an attempt to assess which forms of motivation were most effective in sustaining staff commitment. To get at this very important question of why Grameen staff continue to work in the field under difficult circumstances, managers were asked about the role of managers in sustaining motivation, and officers and non-officers in the field were asked the general question of why Grameen staff continue to work under difficult circumstances. It was thought that staff would give the most honest answers if responding about someone else's, rather than their own, motivation.

Decision-making was examined in the context of centralization or decentralization, with decentralization as a more empowering or participatory design for decision-making. The location of decision-making on the operational level was operationalized by looking at one of the most basic banking decisions: loan approval. Using Mintzberg's definition of decision-making as a multi-step process, the information collection, recommendation, choice and implementation aspects of the loan approval are examined in terms of who participates and who has the final say. Data comes from interviews at several levels, from observations and from documents.

To the extent that jobs are enlarged vertically and horizontally, one would expect greater participation and empowerment of staff at the operating level. This research used the loan decision process as a way of assessing participation in different levels of the process. All the participants and the steps in the process were first identified. The findings were analyzed to determine the diffusion or vertical dimensions of participation.

Finally, planning systems in Grameen Bank are explored. Key characteristics of performance planning and action planning were taken from Mintzberg. Performance planning specifies results but not the means to achieve those results and is an iterative process with both top - down and bottom - up inputs. Action planning specifies the actions to be carried out and is essentially a top - down process. In this sense, performance planning allows greater autonomy, encourages the participation of staff down the hierarchy. Using documents (including the Grameen Guidelines for Budgeting and Planning) and interviews with different levels of managers, the Grameen planning system was analyzed in terms of performance goals, actions specified, and the roles of different levels of the organization in preparing the plan.

SOURCES CONSULTED

Publications

David Abecassis. **Identity, Islam and Human Development in Rural Bangladesh**. Dhaka: Univesity Press Limited, 1990.

Sajeda Amin, "Rural Power Structures and External Service Delivery in Rural Bangladesh: A Case Study in Rajshahi", Report prepared for UNICEF, Dhaka, mimeo, 7 February 1993.

Mary Timney Bailey. "Do Physicists Use Case Studies? Thoughts on Public Administration Research." **Public Administration Review** 52 (January/February 1992): 47-54.

Bangladesh Rural Advancement Committee Donors' Consortium. **Final Appraisal Report on BRAC's Rural Development Programme (1990-1992) and the BRAC Bank Project**, Vol. II. Dhaka: April 1989.

Stephen R. Barley, Gordon W. Meyer, and Debra C. Gash. "Cultures of Culture: Academics, Practitioners and the Pragmatics of Normative Control." **Administrative Science Quarterly** 33, 1988, 24-60.

Joseph E. Black, James S. Coleman, and Lawrence D. Stifel. **Education and Training for Public Sector Management in the Developing Countries**. New York: Rockefeller Foundation, 1976.

Richard C. Box. "An Exmination of the Debate Over Research in Public Administration." **Public Administration Review** 52 (January/February 1992): 62-69.

W. Philip Boyle. "On the Analysis of Organizational Culture in Development Project Planning." Binghamton, N.Y.: Institute for Development Anthropology, 1984.

Tim Brodhead, Brent Herbert-Copley and Anne Marie Lambert. **Bridges of Hope? Canadian Voluntary Agencies and the Third World**. Ottawa: The North South Institute, 1989.

Coralie Bryant and Louise G. White. **Managing Development in the Third World**. Boulder: Westview Press, 1982.

Robert Cassen and Associates. **Does Aid Work? Report to an Intergovernmental Task Force**. Oxford: Clarendon Press, 1987.

Sources

Michael M. Cernea, ed. **Putting People First, Sociological Variables in Rural Development**. New York: Oxford University Press, 1985.

Martha Alter Chen. **A Quiet Revolution: Women in Transition in Rural Bangladesh**. Dhaka: BRAC Prokashana, 1991.

A. Momin Chowdhury. "Appropriate Management Style for Bangladesh." **Management Development** 18 (January-March; April-June 1989): 67-92.

Aditee Nag Chowdhury. **Let Grassroots Speak**. Dhaka: University Press Limited, 1989.

Barbara B. Crane and Jason L. Finkle. "Organizational Impediments to Development Assistance: The World Bank's Population Program." **World Politics** 33 (July 1981): 516-553.

Peter Drucker. **Management: Tasks, Responsibilities, Practices**. New York: Harper & Row, 1985.

Kathleen M. Eisenhardt. "Building Theories from Case Study Research." **The Academy of Management Review** 14 (October 1989): 532-550.

Richard F. Elmore. "Backward Mapping: Implementation Research and Policy Decisions" in **Studying Implementation: Method ological and Administrative Issues**, Walter Williams, 18-35.

Chatham, N.J.: Chatham House Publishers, Inc., 1982.

Milton J. Esman. **Management Dimensions of Development: Perspectives and Strategies**. West Hartford, Conn.: Kumarian Press, 1991.

Wendell L. French and Cecil H. Bell, Jr. **Organization Development: Behavioral Science Interventions for Organization Im provement**. Englewood Cliffs, N.J.: Prentice-Hall, Inc., 1984.

Andreas Fuglesang and Dale Chandler. **Participation as Process - What We Can Learn from Grameen Bank Bangladesh**. Dhaka: Grameen Bank, 1988.

Jean-Claude Garcia Zamor. **Public Participation In Development Planning and Management: Cases from Africa and Asia**. Boulder, Colo.: Westview Press, 1985.

David A. Garvin. **Managing Quality: The Strategic and Competi- tiveEdge**. New York: The Free Press, 1988.

Grameen Bank. **Annual Report 1989**. Dhaka, Grameen Bank, 1990.

Merilee S. Grindle, ed. **Politics and Policy Implementation in the Third World**. Princeton: Princeton University Press, 1980.

Friedrich A. Hayek. "The Pretence of Knowledge". Nobel Memorial Prize Lecture delivered on 11 December 1974 at the Stockholm School of Economics, Stockholm.

Mahabub Hossain. **Credit for Alleviation of Rural Poverty: The Grameen Bank in Bangladesh**. International Food Policy Re search Institute in collaboration with the Bangladesh Institute of Development Studies Research Report 65. International Food Policy Research Institute, 1988.

____. "Labour Force, Employment and Access to Income Earning Opportunities in Bangladesh." Dhaka: Bangladesh Institute of Development Studies [photocopy], 1991.

Ahmed Shafiqul Huque. **Politics and Administration in Bangladesh: Problems and Participation**. Dhaka: University Press Limited, 1988.

Nazrul Islam, Amirul Islam Chowdhury and Khadem Ali. **Evaluation of the Grameen Bank's Rural Housing Programme**. Dhaka: Centre for Urban Studies, University of Dhaka, 1989.

Henry R. Jackelen. "Assessing the Ability of Grameen Bank to Diversify." Pre-formulation Mission Report, BGD/90/C01 Gram een Irrigation Project, May 1988. UNCDF, New York.

Henry R. Jackelen and Elisabeth Rhyne, "Toward a More MarketOriented Approach to Credit and Savings for the Poor" unpublished photocopy n.d.

Mohammad Ali Jinnah. "Management Structure and Leadership Pattern in Bangladesh." **Management Development** 14 (July-September 1985): 21-27.

Bruce F. Johnston and William C. Clark. **Redesigning Rural Development: A Strategic Perspective**. Baltimore: Johns Hop kins University Press, 1982.

David C. Korten. **Community Management: Asian Experience and Perspectives**. West Hartford, Conn.: Kumarian Press, 1986.

____. "Community Organization and Rural Development: A Learning Process Approach." **Public Administration Review** 40 (September-October 1980): 480-512.

Paul R. Lawrence, and Jay W. Lorsch. **Organization and Environ ment: Managing Differentiation and Integration**. Boston: Harvard Business School Press, 1986.

David K. Leonard. "The Political Realities of African Management." Working Paper No. 18 prepared as background material for the

Sources

AID Workshop on the Evaluation of Management in African Agricultural Development Projects. Binghamton: Institute for Development Anthropology, 1984.

_____. **Reaching the Peasant Farmer: Organization Theory and Practice in Kenya**. Chicago: University of Chicago Press, 1977.

Michael Lipton. "Why Poor People Stay Poor" in **Rural Development**, John Harris ed. London: Hutchinson University Library, 1982.

John Madeley. **When Aid Is No Help**. London: Intermediate Technology Publications, 1991.

A.H. Maslow. "A Theory of Human Motivation" in **Readings in Managerial Psychology**, Harold J. Leavitt, Louis R. Pondy and David M. Boje, eds. 20-35. Chicago: University of Chicago Press, 1989.

Mathew B. Miles. "Qualitative Data as an Attractive Nuisance: The Problem of Analysis". **Administration Science Quarterly** 24 (December 1979): 590-601.

Henry Mintzberg. **The Nature of Managerial Work**. New York: Harper and Row, 1973.

_____. **The Structuring of Organizations**. Englewood Cliffs, N.J.: Prentice-Hall, 1979.

Robert S. Mountjoy and Laurence J. O'Toole. "Toward a Theory of Policy Implementation: An Organizational Perspective." **Public Administration Review** 39 (September-October 1979): 465-476.

A.M.A. Muhith. **Bangladesh: Emergence of a Nation**. Dacca: Bangladesh Books International Ltd., 1978.

Swapna Mukhopadhyay. **The Poor in Asia: Productivity-Raising Programmes and Strategies**. Kuala Lumpur: Asian and Pacific Development Centre, 1985.

Gayl D. Ness and Steven R. Brechin. "Bridging the Gap: International Organizations as Organizations." **International Organization** 42 (Spring, 1988): 245-273.

North-South Institute. **Rural Poverty in Bangladesh: A Report to the Likeminded Group**. Ottawa: North-South Institute, 1985.

Peter Oakley. **Projects With People: The Practice of Participation in Rural Development**. Geneva: International Labour Organization, 1991.

Thomas M. Painter. "Development Management in Africa: An Evaluation of the Management Impact of the Niamey Department Development Project (NDD), Niger Republic." Prepared for the

Office of Program and Policy Coordination Center for Development Information and Evaluation of the U.S. Agency for International Development. Binghamton, N.Y.: Institute for Development Anthropology, 1985. Photocopied.

Charles Perrow. **Complex Organizations: A Critical Essay**. New York: Random House, 1986.

Tom Peters. **Thriving on Chaos: Handbook for Management Revolution**. New York: Harper & Row, 1987.

Maurice Punch. **The Politics and Ethics of Fieldwork**. Qualitative Research Methods Series 3. Beverly Hills: Sage Publications, 1986.

Atiur Rahman. "Consciousness-Raising Efforts of Grameen Bank." Dhaka: Bangladesh Institute of Development Studies, 1986. Photocopied.

_____. "Human Responses to Natural Hazards: The Hope Lies in Social Networking." A paper submitted at the 23rd Bengal Studies Conference held in the University of Manitoba, Winnipeg, Canada, 9-11 June 1989. Dhaka: Bangladesh Institute of Development Studies, 1989. Photocopied.

_____. "Participative Management Style of Grameen Bank." A paper presented at a Workshop on Grameen Bank jointly organized by the Bangladesh Bank Training Academy and the Bangladesh Institute of Bank Management, Dhaka, on 27 January 1987. Dhaka: Bangladesh Institute of Development Studies, 1987. Photocopied.

Jowshan A. Rahman. "Grameen Bank: Development from the Bottom." Paper presented at the NGO Forum: End Decade Women's World Conference, Nairobi, Kenya on 17 July 1985. Dhaka: UNICEF, 1985. Photocopied.

Dennis Rondinelli. **Development Projects as Policy Experiments: An Adaptive Approach to Development Administration**. New York: Methuen, 1983.

Constantina Safilios-Rothschild and Simeen Mahmud. **Women's Roles in Agriculture: Present Trends and Potential for Growth**. New York: UNDP and UNIFEM, 1989.

Edgar Schein. **Organizational Culture and Leadership**. San Francisco: Jossey-Bass, 1989.

Sidney Ruth Schuler and Syed M. Hashemi. "Credit Programs, Women's Empowerment, and Contraceptive Use in Rural Bangladesh", **Studies in Family Planning**, Volume 25, No. 2, March

195

April 1994.

Deborah A. Stone. **Policy Paradox and Political Reason**. Glenville, Ill.: Scott, Foresman and Company, 1988.

Paul Streeten. "Poverty Concepts and Measurement." **The Bangladesh Development Studies** 18 (September 1990): 1-18.

Melanie S. Tammen. "Foreign Aid: Treating the Symptoms: Misunderstanding the Microenterprise." **Reason** 22 (June 1990): 40-41.

Judith Tendler. **What Ever Happened to Poverty Alleviation?** A Report Prepared for the Mid-Decade Review of the Ford Foundation's Programs on Livelihood, Employment and Income Generation. New York: Ford Foundation, 1987. Photocopied.

James D. Thompson. **Organizations in Action**. New York: McGraw Hill, 1967.

Krishna K. Tummala, ed. **Administrative Systems Abroad**. New York: University Press of America, Inc., 1982.

Norman Uphoff and Milton J. Esman. **Local Organization For Rural Development in Asia**. Ithaca, N.Y.: Rural Development Committee, Center for International Studies, Cornell University, 1974.

United Nations Fund for Population Activities. **Bangladesh: Programme Review and Strategy Development Report**. New York: UNFPA 1990.

Walter Williams. **Studying Implementation: Methodological and Administrative Issues**. Chatham, N.J.: Chatham House Publishers, Inc., 1982.

World Bank. **Bangladesh: Strategies for Enhancing the Role of Women in Economic Development**. Washington, D.C.: World Bank, 1990.

_____. **Sub-Saharan Africa: From Crisis to Sustainable Growth**. Wasington, D.C.: World Bank, 1989.

Robert K. Yin. **Case Study Research: Design and Methods**. Applied Social Research Methods Series Volume 5. Newbury Park, Calif.: Sage Publications, 1989.

Muhammad Yunus. "On Reaching the Poor." Paper presented at the IFAD Project Implementation Workshop, New Delhi, April 1984. Photocopied.

_____. "Credit for Self-Employment of the Poor." Transcript of the Telephone Press Conference held with Professor Muhammad Yunus in Washington D.C. on 22 July 1987.

_____, ed. **Jorimon and Others: Faces of Poverty**. Dhaka: University Press Limited, 1987.

Key Interviews and Speeches

S. M. Abdullah, Area Manager, Dinajpur Area, Grameen Bank. Interview by author, 9, 10, 11 April 1991, Dinajpur.

Farouk Ahmed, Chief, Monitoring and Evalution, Dinajpur Zonal Office, Grameen Bank. Interview by author, 10 April 1991, Dinajpur.

Babur Ali, Zonal Manager, Bogra Zone, Grameen Bank. Interview by author, 13 December 1991, Bogra.

Dipal Chandra Barua, Deputy General Manager, Administration, Grameen Bank. Interview by author, 23 March 1991, Dhaka tape recorded.

Nurjahan Begum, Principal, Training Institute, Grameeen Bank. Interview by author, 17 March 1991, Dhaka, tape recorded.

Shamsul Alam Khan Chowdhery, Zonal Manager, Dinajpur Zone, Grameen Bank, Interview by author, 7 April 1991, Dinajpur, tape recorded.

Omar Faruque, Branch Manager, Nimgachi Branch, Rayganj Area, Grameen Bank. Interview by author, 12 December 1990, Nimgachi.

Mir Hossain, International Programs, Grameen Bank. Interview by author, December 1990, Dhaka.

Mary Houghton, Shorebank Corporation, Chicago. Interview by author, 12 April 1992, Chicago.

Khandakar Mozammel Huq, General Manager, Grameen Bank. Interview by author, 17 December 1990; 19 April 1991, Dhaka, second interview tape recorded.

Zubairul Huq, Deputy General Manager, Central Accounts, Grameen Bank. Interview by author, 25 April 1991, Dhaka, tape recorded.

Masud Isa, Assistant General Manager, Planning, Grameen Bank. Interview by author, 25 April 1991, Dhaka, tape recorded.

Aminul Islam, Area Manager, Bhuyapur Area, Grameen Bank. Interviews by author, 27-30 April 1991, Bhuyapur.

Nazrul Islam, Zonal Manager, Rangpur Zone, Grameen Bank.

Sources

Interview by author, 6 April 1991, Ranpur.

Mushtaque Khan, Area Manager, Rayganj, Grameen Bank.
Interview by author, 8, 9, 11, 13 December 1990, Nimgachi.

Tajul Islam Mazumder, Impact Area Manager, Save the Children
(USA), Bangladesh. Interviews by author, 20-24 April 1991,
Nasirnagar Area.

Mohammad Mortuza, Deputy General Manager, Monitoring and
Evaluation, Grameen Bank. Interview by author, 17 March
1991, Dhaka, tape recorded.

Habibur Rahman, Branch Manager, Garidaha, Rayganj Area,
Grameen Bank. Interview by author, 13 December 1990,
Garidaha.

Md. Mizan Rahman, Area Manager, Sherpur Area, Grameen Bank.
Interviews by author, 27 March-2 April 1991, Sherpur.

Abdul Rashid, Branch Manager, Fikrabad, Dinajpur Area, Grameen
Bank. Interview by author, 10 April 1991, Fikrabad.

Md. Abdur Razzaque, Assistant General Manager, Establishment,
Grameen Bank. Interviews by author, December 1990, 19
March 1991, Dhaka.

Angela van Rynbach, Country Director, Bangladesh, Save the
Children USA, Dhaka. Interviews by author, October, 16 December 1990, New York and Dhaka.

Md. Shahjahan, Assistant General Manager, Audit, Grameen Bank.
Interview by author, 18, 19 March 1992, Dhaka, tape recorded.

Khalid Shams, Deputy Managing Director, Grameen Bank.
Interview by author, 20 March 1991, Dhaka, tape recorded.

Imamis Sultan, Secretary, Grameen Bank. Interview by author,
12 December 1990, Dhaka.

Maheen Sultan, Resource Person, Secretariat, Grameen Bank.
Interviews by author, December 1990; March and April 1991.

Focus Group Discussions

Zonal Meeting, Bogra Zone, 3 April 1991, tape recorded.
Zonal Meeting, Dhaka Zone, Dhaka, 2 May 1991, tape recorded.
Zonal Meeting, Dinajpur Zone, 8 April 1991, tape recorded.
Zonal Meeting, Rangpur Zone, Rangpur, 6 April 1991, tape
recorded.

Workshops and Meetings

Dinajpur Branch Meeting, Grameen Bank, 9 April 1991, partially
    tape recorded.
Grameen Bank, Sirajganj Area Workshop for Bank Workers,
    December 13, 1990.
Grameen Bank Senior Staff, Meeting with author, December 17,
    1990.

INDEX

Index